WHAT'S YOUR STORY?

D1298488

TOBEN AND JOANNE HEIM

WHAT'S YOUR STORY?

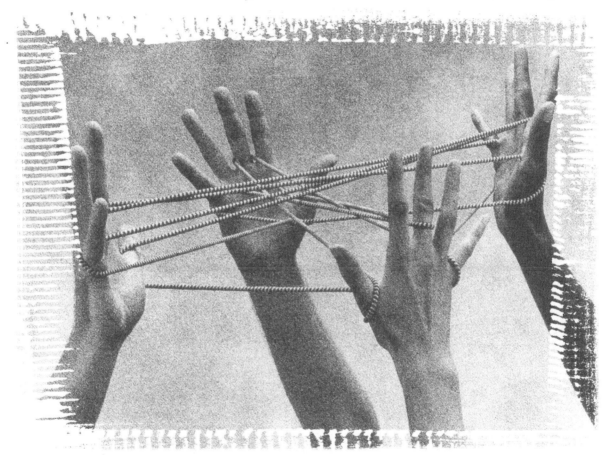

AN INTERACTIVE GUIDE TO BUILDING AUTHENTIC RELATIONSHIPS

PIÑON PRESS

P.O. Box 35007, Colorado Springs, Colorado 80935

Cover illustration by David Diaz

Some of the anecdotal illustrations in this book are true to life and are
included with the permission of the persons involved. All other illustrations are composites of real situations, and any resemblance to people
living or dead is coincidental.

   Heim, Toben, 1970–
        What's your story : an interactive guide to building authentic
   relationships / Toben and Joanne Heim.
           p.   cm.
      ISBN 1-57683-124-8 (pbk.)   1. Interpersonal relations.
   2. Man-woman relationships.
   I. Heim, Joanne, 1972–   . II. Title.
   HQ801.H43   1999
   302—dc21   99-12185
                                                       CIP

Printed in the United States of America

1 2 3 4 5 6 7 8 9 10 11 12 13 14 15 / 05 04 03 02 01 00 99

To Steve and Andrea,
Steve and Michelle,
and Doug and Lisa.
You have taught us the true meaning of community.

Contents

Preface
Telling Your Story—How to Use This Book with a Group 13

Introduction
First Thoughts—What's Your Story? 15

Part One
Where I Came From—Stories About the Past 23

Part Two
Where I Am—Stories About the Present 51

Part Three
Where I'm Going—Stories About the Future 79

Part Four
What I Think—Stories About Values and Opinions 103

Part Five
What I Believe—Stories About Faith 131

About the Authors 155

Acknowledgments

This book couldn't have been written without the help of so many people. We'd especially like to thank Robb, Rebecca, Steve, Michelle, Quentin, and Mitch for their willingness to bare their souls in print. Also thanks to Jim and Sarah for their essays and all the extra time and energy they spent helping us bring this book into being. We wouldn't have wanted to do it without your help.

"The life which is unexamined is not worth living."
—Plato

TELLING YOUR STORY

HOW TO USE THIS BOOK WITH A GROUP

A lot of people will probably go through this book on their own, but for those of you wishing to go through it with a group, here are a few ideas that should help make that a fun and productive experience.

- First, it might be a good idea to find a facilitator. Maybe that's you.
- Find a few friends (or potential friends) to work through the book together. Your enthusiasm will get everyone else excited about it too.
- Set a time (weekly, biweekly, monthly) to get everyone together. It works best to set a regular time to meet and get it scheduled in advance. Everyone is so busy that if you don't set up regular times to meet, it may be difficult or impossible to get everyone together.
- Set some ground rules as a group. Talk about things like purpose (why you're all getting together), participation (make sure everyone has a similar idea of what it means to be part of the group), attendance (how important is it for everyone to be there each time you meet), confidentiality (make sure that what's said in the group stays in the group), and accessibility (how open is everyone to being available to the other members of the group).
- Encourage group members to get together between regular meetings, send E-mail, or make occasional phone calls to each other. This will continue to build those friendships that will make your times together more fun and a little more comfortable for everyone.
- If you sense that someone really isn't into the group or is losing interest, take the time to ask him or her what's up. The reason for the disconnect may be something easy to fix.
- Different people in your group are going to have different communication styles and comfort levels when it comes to sharing their stories. Be sensitive to these differences. You may have to do a little extra work to draw out quiet people or to make sure the more vocal members of the group don't bury them.

After things get going, feel free to let others try their hand at facilitation. That will increase their ownership in the group and will give you a chance to sit back and participate without the responsibility for keeping things moving.

Each chapter in this book has five sections. As a group, decide which of the sections you want to cover each time you get together. You may want to schedule your interactions with the book like this:

Week 1 — Go through a few of the Getting Started questions.

Week 2 — Read and respond to the essay and its questions.

Week 3 — Read and respond to the dialog.

Week 4 — Go through a few of the Next Level questions.

Week 5 — Write down some thoughts in the journal pages and come prepared to share.

You can repeat this pattern for each section of the book, but you can also take the book in smaller chunks or larger ones, depending on how many weeks you want to commit to getting together.

There may be certain chapters that are more interesting to your group than others. Feel free to pick and choose the chapters you'll cover. Regardless of how you decide to structure your time together, keep in mind that when you're covering issues as interesting and personal as people's stories, it may be difficult to get as much done as you'd hoped to with each meeting. If it takes you twice as long to get through a section as you thought it would, that's probably a good thing. It means everyone is really getting into it!

WHAT'S YOUR STORY?

sto·ry \ stor´ē, stōr´ē\ *n* **1** *archaic*: HISTORY
2 a: an account of incidents or events
b: a statement regarding the facts pertinent
to a situation in question

Our lives are compilations of our stories. The stories of where we came from, where we are, where we're going, what we think, and what we believe all work together to make us who we are. At our core, we are walking anthologies made up of the stories of our experiences.

By telling our stories, we open the book of our lives to share with others. And by listening to other people's stories, we learn why they are the way they are.

My (Joanne's) uncle says there's a story behind every story. And he's right. Why does Michelle take marriage so seriously—convinced that "till death do us part" really means just that, no matter what happens? Listen to her talk about her parents' separation and near divorce. How her dad had an affair with another woman and wanted a divorce. How her mom remained faithful to a man who'd been unfaithful, and refused to sign divorce papers. How Michelle felt when she saw her mom struggle to hide tears and bruises. How her parents are in love with each other today.

Why does Mitch struggle with pornography? Why does he still use it when he hates how it makes him feel afterward? Listen to him talk about the first time he was introduced to it. How it was presented as no big deal—just something boys do that can't really hurt anyone. How he vows again and again to leave it alone for good. How he feels when he looks into his wife's eyes and sees the hurt and pain pornography has caused her.

Why is Rebecca always looking for a true friend—one who is loyal, trustworthy, and promises to stick with her through thick and thin? Listen to her talk about her best friends in high school. How—without explanation—they decided they didn't want to be friends anymore. How hurt she felt when the same thing happened in college. How she's learned to forgive and then give, even when she's not getting anything in return.

Taking the time to ask people questions and hear their stories tells you who they are. Explains some of their behaviors. Helps you to be a better friend. Gives you understanding and tolerance for others.

There's a story behind every story. Stories come in layers. One story leads to another. Listening to stories and telling our own takes time. And time isn't something we give freely. Telling our stories is an investment—a wise one. It pays off in friendship, intimacy, and growth.

If you ask me what my friends and I do when we get together, I could answer with any number of things. We eat. We go to movies. We laugh. We watch TV. We play games. We pray. We hang out. And sometimes we cry. But at the heart of it, we tell stories. And while we're telling stories, we're creating new stories together.

When I think back to those moments that make me value friendships, the times friendships deepened and grew, I remember the stories. Stories are at the heart of intimate relationships. And intimacy is what I want—with others and with God. I want others to know me, and I want to know them.

I want to know their stories. And the stories behind those stories. And the stories behind those stories. . . .

What's Your Story? is all about learning how to tell your story and how to listen to the stories others tell. There are some fun questions and some difficult ones. There are essays from people who have asked themselves questions—and struggled to answer honestly. There are journal pages for you to ask yourself questions and practice telling your story. And running throughout the book is dialog—a real conversation that happened as a result of asking real questions.

Telling your story can be scary. It's not easy to let people see you for who you really are. But it's worth it. You learn more about who you are. You learn more about others. And through it all you begin to play a part in the stories of others as you grow and influence each other's thoughts, ideas, and lives.

How This Book Works

What's Your Story? is divided into five different sections—past, present, future, values and opinions, and beliefs. Of course, it's impossible to talk about any of these areas of our lives without some overlap. We can't neatly divide our lives into compartments where our past and our values don't connect. You may find that you have to backtrack at times (or forward track!) within these different sections to answer the questions thoroughly.

Within each section, there's a common set of elements. They're identified by icons so you can follow one element throughout the book if you really like it (or ignore it if that element isn't working for you).

Each section of the book starts with an introduction. This brief section gives an overview of the topic—past, values, future, et cetera—and describes the goal for exploring your stories in this area.

The questions in the Getting Started section are especially great if you're reading this book with a group of friends. They're designed to get you talking and having fun. If you're reading this book on your own, these questions are a way to start thinking about the topic being addressed.

Each section also includes an essay on the topic. The essays are designed to let you get inside someone else's head to see how his or her particular story unfolds. The essay can be an example of how to answer some of the questions or a way to approach a question in a new way. Each essay ends with a few questions to help you apply the writer's story to your own life.

The Next Level is filled with questions designed to dig deep. These questions require more thought than Getting Started questions and can take a lot of time to answer if you really get into them.

Throughout each section is a real conversation. While writing the book, we gathered together a group of people (see the cast of characters following this section) to talk about these different issues. You'll get to see how they interacted with the material and what can happen when you tell your story within a group.

Sometimes it's hard to tell your story without some practice. Journal pages are included in each section to give you space to explore your stories and how they've affected your life.

DIALOG CAST OF CHARACTERS

Michelle:

Nickname: None. I hate nicknames.

Occupation: accountant

Where you live: Colorado Springs, Colorado

Favorite book: There are too many to pick just one.

Most influential person in your life, and why: Probably my mom. She has taught me so much about how to be a good person, wife, friend, and everything else you could imagine.

What you look for in a friend: honesty, integrity, and a crazy-wild sense of humor

Where you meet friends: church, primarily, and work—oh, and those male strip clubs I frequent

Most significant relationship: my husband, Steve

Hidden talent: acting

Favorite subject in school: history—I used to want to teach history.

Likes: reading, writing, hiking, watching snow fall, going to movies with my friends

Dislikes: pretentious people, my neighbor's dogs

Ideal friend: my husband

Something you wish you could do: travel all over the world

Something you'd change about yourself: I'd take more risks in life instead of planning and analyzing everything so thoroughly.

Steve:

Nickname: Depends on who is calling. "Z" to my best friends, "Tuffy" to others

Occupation: construction loan coordinator

Where you live: Colorado Springs, Colorado

Favorite book: anything by Louis L'Amour or J. R. Tolkien

Most influential person in your life, and why: My oldest brother. My dad died when I was three months old, and my mother never remarried, so I was missing the dad role model. My brother filled that role and taught me a lot about life and how to act toward others and situations.

What you look for in a friend: sense of humor is a big one, slightly off-kilter personality, someone who I feel I can trust with my life

Where you meet friends: bars, theaters, houses of burlesque

Most significant relationship: my wife and lover (same person—in Chinese, the word is *airen*, signifying wife/lover)

Hidden talent: Most people don't know that I can play the trombone, and I love to sing. Neither is necessarily a talent, unless you do them well, but I feel that I do both of these very well . . . at least the singing.

Favorite subject in school: math in high school, Chinese in college

Likes: hiking, reading, biking, snow sports, water sports, computer games, my dog

Dislikes: bad drivers, slow movies, American "Chinese" food, dogs that won't obey, people who won't take the time to get to know the real me before judging me completely

Ideal friend: someone I can share every aspect of my life with and know that I will not be judged by them (at least not too harshly), and they can do the same with me, and someone I can be accountable to and for

Something you wish you could do: Other than own a whole mountain, I'd like to be able to take a month and hike back from deep in the mountain wilderness, surviving on what I can find.

Something you'd change about yourself: I am way too competitive—even in things that don't matter. In those things, I'd like to lessen the competitive attitude.

Rebecca:

Nickname: Reba

Occupation: mental health assessor

Where you live: Federal Way, Washington

Favorite Book: This Present Darkness by Frank Peretti

Most influential person in your life, and why: My parents are the most influential people in my life for the obvious reasons, but also because they are the reason I have been blessed with such a fortunate life. They instilled in me values that are becoming more and more rare today, and they introduced me to Jesus.

What you look for in a friend: honesty, sincerity, compassion, loyalty, love

Where you meet friends: school (in the past) and church

Most significant relationship: Hate to be trite, but Jesus; he's the one constant, unfailing, faithful example I can have.

Hidden talent: I can whistle with my rolled tongue.

Favorite subject in school: without a doubt, art

Likes: surprises, winter, tennis

Dislikes: mustard, mushrooms, laundry

Ideal friend: Robb, because he's all the things I look for in a friend (see above)

Something you wish you could do: play an instrument

Something you'd change about yourself: I'm too quick to judge.

Robb:

Nickname: Dedon

Occupation: counselor on a psych unit and MSW (Masters of Social Work) student at the University of Washington

Where you live: Federal Way, Washington

Favorite Book: The Chosen by Chaim Potok

Most influential person in your life, and why: Paul Hargreaves. He was a good friend and youth director in my church. He had more impact on me than I think he ever knew.

What you look for in a friend: laughter and fun

Where you meet friends: work, and through other friends

Most significant relationship: Rebecca—my wife

Hidden talent: commercial aircraft identification from ground level

Favorite subject in school: Spanish

Likes: coffee, travel, and people

Dislikes: scatting, tofu, and passive-aggressive communication styles

Ideal friend: Tim

Something you wish you could do: pilot commercial jets

Something you'd change about yourself: be more spontaneous

Sarah:

Nickname: none

Occupation: account rep for technology company

Where you live: The basin of hell. Okay, only when it's a hundred degrees for about three months running. Otherwise I love it in San Antonio, Texas.

Favorite book: I have to pick one? *The Waves* by V. Woolf (ha ha, don't I seem literary?; but it's true, that would be it if I had to pick one). Of course, I'd like to add *A Prayer for*

Owen Meany, The Heart of Darkness, Great Expectations; the list is long and illustrious.

Most influential person in your life, and why: Okay, it's Reba, but don't tell her I said so or it'll go straight to her head. The fact that she's my sister only makes our friendship stronger. She pushes me around (in a good way) and continually challenges me to be a better person.

What you look for in a friend: irreverence, a sense of humor, unconditional acceptance (as in lack of judgment), and the ability to have interesting conversations

Where you meet friends: church, work

Most significant relationship: see influential person above

Hidden talent: blowing smoke rings

Favorite subject in school: literature, followed closely by math, followed closely by chemistry/physics

Likes: life, adventure, affirmation, reading, reading, reading, learning new things, taking risks

Dislikes: boredom, easy answers, judgment, three months when the temp is over a hundred degrees

Ideal friend: Ally McBeal

Something you wish you could do: snowboard

Something you'd change about yourself: my absolute lack of patience

Quentin:

Nickname: Q

Occupation: international sales guy

Where you live: a one-bedroom hovel

Favorite book(s): Brothers Karamazov by Fyodor M. Dostoyevski, *Till We Have Faces* by C. S. Lewis, *The Weight of Glory* by C. S. Lewis, *Confessions* by Saint Augustine, *Sir Gibbie* by George MacDonald, *Desiring God* by John Piper

Most influential person in your life, and why: I grew up in the same town that my grandparents lived in. My grandfather was a pastor, and some of my earliest memories are of the church he pastored. Interestingly enough, I remember very little about the actual sermons he gave, but recall vividly the times we spent together and the life lessons he taught me when we were together. From an early age he taught me not to rely on "Sunday school answers" to build my belief system. Not that they were wrong, but he wanted to be sure that I *knew* what I believed and wasn't just regurgitating pat answers to the questions being asked. He challenged my belief structure, such as it was as a child, in a safe environment that gave room for heated discussion, lengthy arguments, and even a little yelling without the risk of harm to the relationship. He wasn't perfect either and wasn't afraid to let me see his imperfections. I saw how he genuinely cared for others and sacrificed for the good of others (and enjoyed every minute of it). He died more than fifteen years ago, but I still remember the times we spent together.

What you look for in a friend: I look for friends who I can learn from. My close friendships have grown through many stages and tend to be long-term.

Where you meet friends: Uh . . . good question!

Favorite subject in school: English

Likes: my Palm Pilot, the new VW bug, ugly postcards, Ska, cheap shoes, and Baby Gap

Dislikes: bills, colored contacts, finding character references, having to dig someone else's lint out of the lint trap at the laundromat

Something you wish you could do: be Hank Hill, climb Mount Everest

Something you'd change about yourself: I would like to be more organized. I don't mean learning organizational skills, I mean I wish that I had innate organizational skills that others seem to possess which makes being organized EASY for them. I enjoy having several projects going at once, I enjoy coming up with ideas and getting things started, but the energy it takes to maintain them and the frustration level I usually experience seeing them to completion takes its toll on me. I find that the first area of my life that's negatively affected by this is my relationships, which adds to my frustration. Why do I say that relationships are so important to me if they are always the first thing to go when I get busy?

Toben:

Nickname: none

Occupation: trade sales manager for a publishing company—that means I work with bookstores and people who work with bookstores.

Where you live: Colorado Springs, Colorado also referred to as Colo Spgs

Favorite book: Life After God by Douglas Coupland (and everything else he has written)

Most influential person in your life, and why: I have been influenced by a number of people: my wife, and parents—but the first person who comes to mind is my uncle, Jim. He is a mentor and a friend.

What you look for in a friend: fun, low maintenance, good self-esteem, and a commonality of interest

Where you meet friends: I meet friends everywhere I go. I like people so much that I have a hard time not making friends wherever I am.

Most significant relationship: My God, my wife, and my daughter, in that order—although I don't always act like it.

Hidden talent: My hidden talent is so hidden that even I don't know what it is.

Favorite subject in school: Does student government count as a subject?

Likes: I love my friends. They energize me. I can be in the middle of a totally flat day and get with my friends and the lights just come on. Everything seems to get better when I'm around them.

Dislikes: being alone

Ideal friend: One part of me wants to say, "my wife, Joanne," but a less virtuous side of me wants to say, "Bill Gates."

Something you wish you could do: make everyone feel important

Something you'd change about yourself: view myself as a little less important than I usually do

Joanne:

Nickname: none (although my husband now calls me Dairy Queen since our baby was born!)

Occupation: editor, mom

Where you live: in a house that's cozy and filled with colors and things I love

Favorite book: That's a tough one—I have lots of favorites. They include *Anne of Green Gables, The Secret Garden*, and the *Chronicles of Narnia*.

Most influential person in your life, and why: my mom—she is a true lady—a godly woman who loves her family and whose inner beauty is apparent to everyone she meets

What you look for in a friend: honesty, fun, loyalty, someone who loves me despite my faults

Where you meet friends: all over—childbirth classes, snowboard shops, church, work

Most significant relationship: with my daughter, Audrey—she teaches me to give without expecting to receive, and to love no matter what

Hidden talent: I can break an apple in half with my bare hands.

Favorite subject in school: French

Likes: reading, thunderstorms, rocky road ice cream, autumn

Dislikes: needles, Brussels sprouts, people who are late, snakes (ugh!)

Ideal friend: We can talk for hours or sit silently—and be comfortable doing both.

Something you wish you could do: go without sleep and not be grumpy

Something you'd change about yourself: not sweat the little stuff, and roll with the punches

PART ONE:
WHERE I CAME FROM

STORIES ABOUT THE PAST

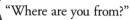 "Where are you from?"

It seems like a pretty simple question. I (Joanne) was born in California, lived in Colorado, Alabama, England, Colorado again, Washington, and France. Then back to Colorado—again.

Ask me about my family. I'm the oldest of two. My parents have been married for almost thirty years. My dad works; my mom doesn't. My sister and I usually get along pretty well.

Ask me about school. A straight-A student from the start. Editor of my college paper. Finished school in three years with two majors.

Finally, ask me what I regret. I regret not being able to be honest at the time about things that really hurt me. I regret that I was sometimes scared to try new things and missed once-in-a-lifetime opportunities because of it. I regret that I didn't always trust my instincts.

In *The Sound of Music,* when Maria taught the von Trapp kids to sing, she said the beginning is a very good place to start. Where we come from shapes who we are. It explains things about who we are today and why we think the way we do.

Stories about the past come in layers, each one revealing more about who we are. Questions about the past can touch the surface or dig deep. And sometimes it's not just the questions, but how we answer them.

If you ask, I can tell you that my first apartment was on my college campus, and it had one bedroom, the smallest kitchen imaginable, and a great view

past \past\ *n* 1: a time

gone by 2: something

that happened or was

done in the past

of the woods. Or I can tell you about how it felt to have my own place for the first time. The fun of having an illegal cat for a few weeks—one that fell into the toilet in the middle of the night because the toilet didn't have a lid. The pride of having people over to dinner at my home—especially when the dinner turned out well. The embarrassment when it didn't turn out so well.

Sharing stories about our past is a key step in building relationships. Our stories provide a foundation for understanding who we are and often give us common ground with others.

I think about my closest friend from high school. Ann and I didn't always spend a lot of time together, but we clicked. We seemed to agree about a lot and approached things from the same direction. As we talked about where we'd come from, we found out just how similar our stories were.

We both grew up in Air Force families. We'd both lived in Montgomery, Alabama—just a year or two apart—while our dads attended war college. From there, both of our families moved to England. We were stationed at different bases, but we both went to British school, took English riding lessons, and traveled extensively throughout Europe. We could relate to each other's experience of British school lunches. (Trust me—you don't want to know!)

Because we'd both moved so much while growing up, we knew how tough it can be to make friends. And because our dads were both pretty high up in the Air Force, we knew about the pressure to be a "model" family.

Telling stories about our past provided a strong foundation for our friendship. Finding similarities in our past made it easy to talk to each other when we struggled with everything from growing up to feeling left out when other friends talked about knowing each other all their lives.

Telling stories about the past isn't a one-time event. Ann and I still talk about those things that we have in common from childhood. It reinforces the bond we have and is just plain fun.

As you think about your past, start thinking about those stories that help explain what makes you who you are today.

First things first...

Firsts can be fun to talk about because they bring back memories. But they can also be painful. If your first broken heart happened ten or twenty years ago, maybe you can laugh about it now. But if it happened last month, maybe you still feel like crying about it.

Memories are really stories about the past. Think about your first date, your first apartment, or your first car. Chances are you don't think of a quick, one-word answer. Those things all happened in a context and are part of a story. Maybe your first car was a 1967 Dodge Dart. Big deal. I'd rather hear about the first time you hit the road in that beauty. How did it feel to travel somewhere in your own car for the first time? Where did you go? Did you have to work a couple of summer jobs to pay for your car, or did your grandma give it to you for your sixteenth birthday?

Think about some of these firsts. What stories come to mind? What feelings come rushing back?

Memory	Vacation	House
Kiss	Failure	Record album
Date	Success	Big purchase
Apartment	Day of school	Broken heart
Friend	Day you skipped school	Sleep over
Fear	Job	Big scare
Pet	Crush	Long car trip
Death	Book	Betrayal
Car	Movie	
Fight	Concert	

"My First Apartment"

by Sarah Snelling

*The events of our lives happen in a sequence in time,
but in their significance to ourselves, they find their own order.*
—Eudora Welty

I've always been skeptical about people who respond to an open-ended question with a simple answer. When you ask me about my first apartment, conflicting pictures flash in my mind. Often we require ourselves to think linearly; therefore, "first" usually means first chronologically. But what I consider to be my first apartment was really my fourth.

Chronologically, my first apartment was in a dorm on campus. My husband and I rented it for the first six months we were married, while I was finishing school. Living in one of the very few apartments on campus had its benefits. We didn't have to pay utilities. We didn't have to drive to campus every day. And we could easily hang out with friends. Unfortunately, it was in a dorm. We could hear everything above and below us. And we had very little privacy.

The bedroom was barely big enough to hold a bed and a dresser. The living room was just as small, and we had absolutely no cupboard space. The strange thing was that in our barely six-hundred square feet of space, we had a fireplace. It was cozy and perfect for a first place to live. When I got a job, we decided to move so I could be separated from a campus environment and have space enough for him to study if I was watching TV.

Talk about moving from little to much. The next apartment was considerably better than the first. Two bedrooms, two bathrooms, tons of space. Everything was better—except we still had no cupboard space (what is it about apartments and cupboard space?). We ended up storing half of the platters and place mats in the linen closet. We signed a one-year lease—not a lot to be optimistic about. I never thought twice that we wouldn't be happily living there for the two years it would take for Justin to finish school.

There's too much to say about that year. No one explains to you in college that everything changes when you get a job. No one tells you not to get a credit card. No one gives you crash courses in budgeting or marriage. Or, if they try, it's done in such a condescending manner that it's unpalatable to those of us who like to make up our own minds about things. We'd gripe every time some adult snickered and made a comment about the "real" world. We thought we knew everything, and our world seemed quite "real" indeed.

I never anticipated that a job could make me so tired. I was in bed by 9:00 every night, falling asleep exhausted and waking up in the morning—still exhausted—at 6:00. Justin could never figure out how I got so tired when I was "just sitting at a desk and talking on the phone" for eight hours a day. It was hard for me to explain the pressure of working in a business environment. There was no time to sit and contemplate literature or art or math. Decisions had to be made quickly and with determination. Justin's life—college life—had the advantage of a varying schedule with free hours spread out over the week. My job allowed me one hour—lunch—of free time per day. It was difficult enough to get used to these pressures without the additional pressure of trying to communicate with my spouse what I was feeling.

Justin wanted me to sit up late and talk with him after his papers were written, his reading assignments completed. On the surface, it was a reasonable request. Married people need to communicate, but we couldn't find a time when both of us were able to do that.

I turned off and quit trying because I was tired. It was easier just to slip into a world of peaceful coexistence. I felt exhausted by the effort to be a professional all day long. I already had to spend too much time pretending to have it all together. If I fell apart or started to admit fear, I wasn't going to get the support I needed at home. Justin wouldn't just listen to my frustrations about work. He wanted to solve my problems and tried to come up with solutions when all I wanted was to hear, "It'll be all right." Not for lack of love, but for lack of understanding, we began to grow apart.

Because we had moved to a "luxury" apartment, and both of us were horrible with money, we started getting into debt. We were sinking deeper into the hole as each month passed. By January of the following year, our marriage had sunk into that same hole. We shut each other out. I stayed at work later and later and had drinks afterward with my colleagues. There was a special camaraderie between us as coworkers that made it easier to be with them than to go home to my husband, who understood nothing about my job. We could moan and groan about all the things that drove us nuts and then walk away. We weren't looking to make all the problems go away, but to get a little perspective on things.

Justin spent time with other students—studying or just hanging out. I tried to be accommodating, even to the point of hanging out with the same friends he was spending time with. It wasn't working. I felt like a complete failure and feared the worst—that we were headed straight for divorce. I was determined not to let it happen. I kept convincing myself that if we could just get through the next couple of months until summer, we could fix it.

I was wrong.

The last weekend in April, I was feeling particularly miserable about the gap in our marriage. Justin was out of town and I went to hang out with friends. I walked into their house and saw my best friend, Kym. She immediately left the room.

When I went to find her, she was sitting on the bathroom floor, obviously upset.

Quietly, I sat on the edge of the tub and asked her what was wrong. She looked up at me and said, "I can't tell you."

I said, "Kym, you can tell me anything."

She looked at me with anguish and answered, "All right, but if I tell you, you have to be ready to hear it." I swallowed hard.

I knew this conversation could never take place in the house with so many people there. We grabbed shoes and headed out to walk the campus. One hundred and fifty feet from the house, she sucker-punched me. "I'm having an affair with Justin."

I stopped and bent over. At first I thought I would throw up. It seemed an appropriate response. Instead I laughed . . . an "I don't allow myself to cry," "This is not my life," "Who the hell do you think you are" kind of laugh. My best friend was sleeping with my husband. *My husband!* In my world, there are things you just don't do—and sleeping with someone else's husband is at the top of the list. There's no excuse for it. I was shocked into complete dysfunction. We started walking again while I tortured her for details. For some sick reason, I wanted to hear it all. I couldn't help myself; I was a voyeur in my own life story. Finally I'd had enough. She drove me back to my place.

"What are you going to do?" she asked.

"Well, Justin has the car or I'd go see my parents." She volunteered her car.

I thought about leaving right then, but decided to wait until morning.

I drove for three hours alternating between nausea, shock, denial, and anger. But I didn't cry—until I got home. Then I broke down.

My parents helped me a lot but never once told me what to do. They helped me look at several options, and by the time I left, I was ready to confront him. I wasn't planning to throw all of his clothes on the lawn, but to see if we could work it out and stay together.

Still, I'm not proud of my behavior when I confronted Justin. In some ways I wanted to make him pay for the pain he was causing. I made him tell me the truth. I kicked him out for one night and then let him back in. Again and again, I asked him to come back, to put time into the marriage. He alternated between begging for forgiveness and cold, hurtful accusations that all of this was somehow my fault. We stayed together for six weeks. We fought and screamed and cried, and eventually I got tired of it.

We separated in June. We'd been married for a year and a half. To this day, I am afraid to sign a one-year lease.

I'd just become friends with another woman who was in the same boat (divorcing her husband), so we decided to rent an apartment together—number three. In my eyes, this was a lateral move. While we now had two bedrooms and only one bathroom, we gained a washer and dryer and a two-car garage. And, for the first time, I found an apartment with adequate cupboard space.

My money problems began to dissipate. I started paying my credit card bills on time and even had money in the bank (only a couple hundred dollars, but it was a nice cushion).

My roommate and I were quite the pair—immobilized by the shock of ending our respective marriages and afraid of the future. We celebrated our new-found freedom in the most unhealthy ways we could find. I invested in disastrous friendships. I'd spend Friday nights drunk and Saturdays hung over. I started thinking about California. I was happy in California. Okay, so not *happy*, but alive. I longed to be alive again. I wanted to feel and to be affected by life.

Two of my friends got promoted and moved to California. I visited them in September and got the fever. I wanted a change. I'd lived in the same city for more than five years and I was getting antsy for a move. I pressured my company for that move. When they didn't comply, I left them to join another company with a job pending in California.

I moved in the winter of 1996 and spent forty hours looking for an apartment over a three-day period. It was a frightening experience. Anyone who has tried to get an apartment in Northern California will tell you the experience borders on the scene from *When Harry Met Sally* when Harry talks about combining the obituaries with the "For Rent" section. The Bay Area has about a 1 percent vacancy rate, which means there are apartments available, but only in the scariest neighborhoods. I arrived steeled for the long search, but unable to absorb any of it. I was a year and a half out of college, twenty-three years old, divorced, and numb. Moving to California wasn't the best choice I could have made, but I was running back to what I knew. I'd graduated from high school there and went back to prove that California could make me happy. How wrong could I be?

I finally settled on what I thought was a great deal. Sure the rent was $775 a month, the apartment was on the ground floor with a door easily accessible to anyone who wanted to break in, had a kitchen with laughable amounts of cupboard space, and pets were out of the question. Did I mention that it was only a thousand feet away from the train tracks? But it had the biggest closet I've ever seen. I took it without hesitation. About a month later, landlords everywhere started raising rents (not price-gouging, they protested, just good business)—I was glad I had signed a six-month lease.

I knew I wanted to live alone. I was tired of sharing my space. I wanted to go home at the end of the day and watch TV—alone; cook dinner—alone;

and sleep—alone. I figured everything would start to happen so fast that I'd have dozens of friends calling me. I moved into my apartment with high hopes.

The first night I stayed in my apartment, I hardly slept at all. There was a gas wall heater that banged every time it came on. When it was off, I swore I could hear someone walking around in my living room. I got up to check the deadbolt on the door at least twenty times. People would walk by outside and I imagined they were going to attempt a break-in. Commuter trains rolled by until 1:00 A.M. I finally gave up, turned on the TV, and slept fitfully on my couch.

I settled into a pattern. Go to work, come home, watch movies, sleep. The weekends were worse. I'd go home on Friday and sometimes not leave again until Monday morning. I'd lie on the couch with the shades closed, watching TV. I'd get on the Internet and hang out in endless chat rooms. The phone wouldn't ring. California was not making me happy.

I'm not an introvert by nature. I thrive on interaction. Yet here I was shutting myself away from the world for fear of being hurt again. The loneliness filled my life and I was sinking into numb depression. Something had to give. I couldn't spend the rest of my life depressed about the fact that I had no life. I saw the future and it scared me. I imagined that I could stay in my apartment alone for six weeks and no one would know the difference. If I didn't get out of this spiral now, it was never going to happen.

After about three months of haze, I kicked myself out of bed and started doing things on the weekends. I started reading again. I went to cafes and drank lattés. I sat in the sun in the park and read books. I went to movies by myself. It was hard and I didn't immediately feel better. Like coming in out of the cold, the first breath of warmth is a little startling and painful. Finally, I went back to church.

Sundays now involved service in the morning and a singles' group in the evening. If nothing else, it was an excuse to get out of bed on the weekends. I grew up in the church, but I'd been avoiding it. After all, church always challenged me to live. I knew that I had to start making the choice to be more than just success-ful at work. I had to be good at life. Being good at life is challenging. It's much too easy just to avoid living—to stay inside a dark apartment and watch television. I opened the curtains. I made friends. I started living.

The truth of the matter is that California didn't make me happy. I had to make a choice. I had to choose whether to live, happy and single, or to die emotionally. I couldn't rely on relationships to change my life. I couldn't rely on places to change my life. I had to learn how to live as an adult. No one was going to outline the process for me; it was something I had to live. Every day, I made the choice to get out of bed and go to work and come home.

That is why this was My First Apartment. Just as I had to become responsible for choosing to live, I had to make these choices alone. Alone, I choose to live fully and creatively, to share my life with good friends, to take risks, to take walks and see plays, to read great books and go to museums, to love my family, and to rest in God's arms.

How do you feel when people talk to you about the "real" world?

Sarah said that at one point she "turned off and quit trying" because she was tired. Have you ever felt that way? How did it affect your relationships?

Have you ever had a friend tell you something that "sucker-punched" you? Describe it. How did you respond?

Sarah talks about the pattern she settled into that helped her avoid really living. Have you ever found yourself stuck in a pattern like that? What did you do about it?

Sarah concludes by saying that she had to make a choice about how her life would be. What are you choosing (either on purpose or by default) for your life?

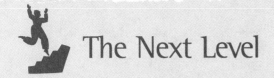

The Next Level

What do you miss about childhood?

What did you want to be when you grew up? Why?

What's one of the hardest things you've had to ask forgiveness for? What made it so difficult?

Describe your family.

Who was your favorite teacher? What made him or her special?

Who was your first friend? What do you remember about that friendship?

If you could change one thing about your family, what would it be?

What kinds of vacations did your family take? Which one stands out to you? Why?

How did your family celebrate holidays?

What are some of your family's traditions?

Did your family move when you were growing up? What was that like for you?

Who's the first person you ever hurt?

What's the worst thing that ever happened to you?

What were some of the rules in your house when you were growing up?

What is something you regret? Why?

If you have siblings, did you get along when you were growing up? Why, or why not? What changed as you grew into adulthood?

Did your parents work when you were young? How did that affect your family?

Is there a mistake in your past that you're glad you made? Why?

How did your family spend time together? Was it usually centered around an activity, a conversation, or nothing at all?

Did you get an allowance when you were young? Did you have to do something for it, or was it automatically yours?

What was your family's view of debt?

What national events do you remember as a child? Why do they stand out to you?

Describe a time when you felt completely safe.

How did your family celebrate birthdays when you were growing up?

If you could change one thing about your past, what would it be?

Describe a time when you felt lonely. How did you work past it?

Do you remember the first time you stayed home alone? What was it like?

What do you remember about school when you were a child?

Describe a time when you felt loved.

What kinds of chores did you have to do when you were growing up?

Nineteenth century artist John La Farge, said, "The past, though it cannot be relived, can always be repaired." Have you had to repair something in the past? Is there anything in your past that needs repairing? What steps can you take to do so?

Marcus Valerius Martial said, "To be able to look back upon one's past life with satisfaction is to live twice." Do you agree with this statement? Why, or why not? Have you ever "lived twice" like this? Describe it.

Simone Weil said, "The destruction of the past is perhaps the greatest of all crimes." Have you ever destroyed part of your past? Describe it. Do you think you've suffered for it, or not?

Toben: What's one of your earliest memories?

Q: Well, this morning I . . .

Steve: My mom locked the porch door so I couldn't streak after my bath. I was four or five at the time.

Q: Was this something you really wanted to do?

Steve: Every day after the bath, I'd jump up before Mom toweled me off and I'd run around the house naked. One day she locked the screen door so I couldn't run outside, and I cried.

Toben: At least she didn't lock it after you got out! You're out there naked screaming, "Mom, let me back in the house!"

I remember we had a house when I was little – it seemed so huge to me. It had a bamboo thicket growing in the corner and we'd go play in there. And there was a swing outside under the patio cover and we could swing outside – even when it was raining. It seemed like it was thirty feet up to me. I was only three or four. Then we'd go inside and watch "Electric Company."

Michelle: I remember arguing with my sister when I was little because I wanted to watch "Sesame Street" and she wanted to watch "Happy Days." Little did I understand that "Happy Days" was the cooler show. But I really wanted to watch "Sesame Street," and I remember throwing a tantrum in the family room.

Rebecca: I remember going to visit my mom in the hospital when she had my little sister, Hannah. I remember Mom held Hannah out the window from the fifth floor when we drove into the hospital parking lot.

Sarah: We couldn't go into the hospital because they didn't allow children to go inside.

Toben: So she hung the baby out the window?

Rebecca: We thought she did! Years later we talked about it and what really happened was that mom held her *up* to the window. But we remember her holding Hannah *out* the window – which was the preferable scenario for Sarah and me. Hannah was born the day before Valentine's Day, and we went up there and brought Mom a big box of chocolates in the shape of a heart. I was almost three and a half.

Q: Probably one of my earliest memories was when my younger brother was adopted. I was four years old and an only child until then. I remember it was the end of November and I think we had a Christmas tree up. My parents brought my brother home, and I thought that's how babies came. I'm sure my parents talked to me about it beforehand, but I just remember them bringing home someone new for me to play with.

Toben: I remember when my parents adopted my sister, Noelle. I was only two and a half, and those memories are all very, very vague. But I remember we picked her up and went to Bob's Big Boy and had breakfast. I don't know why that stands out. Maybe because of the giant Big Boy holding the hamburger.

Robb: I think one of my earliest memories is getting in trouble. I was pretty sneaky and doing things that I probably wasn't supposed to be doing. We lived in California at the time, and my sister and I had to take a nap every day. We had these bright orange comforters on our beds. After putting us down, Mom would vacuum. We would sneak out and steal Oreos and put them under the comforter to eat them. But we'd usually fall asleep. I remember the time Mom came in and there were crushed Oreos everywhere in the beds. I got in trouble for that.

Joanne: What are your memories of your parents from that age?

Robb: My dad was a really fun guy. When he came home from work we'd go out and play in the back yard or ride bikes. He did all kinds of stuff with us. My mom was home during the day, so when Dad came home, we did things with him. He'd take us swimming after work to give Mom a break. He wanted to be very much involved in my life and always wanted to spend time with us. I take that with me—I think about wanting to be available and there for my kids. Any job that I do isn't as important as our kids would be.

Joanne: I remember my mom always doing really special things with me. I remember getting dressed up to go to Marie Callender's to have pie. I wouldn't leave the house without a purse and gloves and beads—and Mom was okay with that.

Toben: I remember going to the office with my dad. I thought the office was the coolest place.

Joanne: When I was about seven or eight my dad taught at the United States Air Force Academy. During the summer, I can remember going to work with him. He had this huge table and I'd climb up on it to color. He had rulers and markers and airplanes hanging down from the ceiling. It made work seem really fun.

Michelle: I remember going to work with my dad at the university. There are few things I remember doing with my dad, but I remember that. The best thing was to go and see the animals. He was in the psychology department and they had rabbits and mice for experiments. He would take me and do tests on me too! His grad students would talk to me and I'd always get pop and a candy bar afterward. That was the only time I ever got candy bars. Those are really the only memories I have of Dad when I was really young.

When Robb talked about his dad always doing fun stuff with them, I can't remember my dad being at home. I know he wasn't a workaholic, but when I think of home, I think of my mom. I remember her sewing and cooking and being there for us.

Toben: Do you ever look at pictures of your parents when you were a little kid and think, *They're so young!*

Rebecca: Yes, but they seemed so old to me then! Even though they were in their twenties.

Sarah: They did young things though. And they seemed to be muddling through a lot. Everything was very structured in our lives. It wasn't oppressive; it was just structured. You'd come home from school and play until dinner time. Then help put dinner on the table. After dinner, we'd play games together. If the "Muppets" were on, we'd watch that together. By 7:00 we were bathed and in bed. We always had a bedtime. My parents would come in and read a story to us and then we had to go to sleep at 7:00 or 7:30 every night. It didn't seem oppressive or anything. It's just the way life was.

Rebecca: It was nice as a little kid because it was predictable. You talk to people now — friends who didn't have a predictable life as a child — and everything seemed so chaotic to them.

Toben: My parents didn't structure my life. Because my sister had so many psychological problems and everything was so weird with her, I think they felt like imposing structure was a bad thing. They wanted me to do what I needed to do to get through that difficult time. But I think you're right. Some of that structure is a positive thing.

Robb: Looking back, does it seem chaotic?

Toben: It was totally chaotic. If I lacked one thing as a kid it was a sense of peace or a sense of order. Our home was always crazy. Noelle started going to therapy when she was five. She'd always been a difficult kid for my parents to deal with. Until I went to college, Noelle provided an underlying tension to everything our family did. It provided so much of the motivation for what we did. When I had school vacations, Mom and Dad would send me away to my aunt and uncle's house so I would have some peace and quiet away from her.

Robb: I think there's a part of every one of us that still wants that structure — we still need it. It may not be that noticeable because we all have our lives and our jobs and we fill our lives with a lot of stuff. But I know there are times when I just want to stay home and get back to the basics of some normal things—to create some of that structure because life seems so chaotic.

Toben: It gets so exhausting. Sarah, you travel a lot. What's that like?

Sarah: I never have the same week from week to week. And for me that causes a lot of stress. I've been doing this now for about eighteen months, and it started to drive me crazy about six months into it. I have weeks when I'm at home and I don't know what to do when I get home at night. I get home at 5:30 or 6:00 and I'm not in a hotel room. I don't necessarily want to turn on the TV and tune out. I don't have to go out to dinner with anyone or be entertaining. There's no minibar. I'm antsy and I have to run around.

Right now, I'm trying to quit smoking. When I'm at home at night, I don't have anything else to fill up my time. And so it helps pass the time. I can go through the day without smoking just fine, but I come home at night and it's two hours and I'm smoking.

Michelle: I really relate to that a lot. I may not be out of town as much, but it's a different client, going to a different place, every week. It's coming home at 7:00 or 8:00 or 9:00 or 10:00 at night and getting there at 7:00 in the morning. It's draining because it's not a consistent thing, and it's just so much time.

I think of my mom being able to do those things like cooking and cleaning. Just to clean my house would be such a great thing! I just don't have the time, and when I do have the time it's the last thing I want to do. I just want to sit.

The ideal life for me would be like "Leave It to Beaver." I'm the mom and get up, send the kids off to school, and do stuff around the house until everyone comes home.

Toben: Was that how growing up was for you?

Michelle: Kind of. I was in junior high when my mom started going back to college to get her bachelor's degree. Then she got her master's degree. She started working—teaching college—when I was in high school.

But I also remember being sent outside because my parents had to have a talk—my dad was going to move out. I was about five years old. Saturday night was bath night, and I remember my dad yelling at my mom. I don't remember what he said. Just yelling. He stormed out of the bathroom and I heard this loud crash in the kitchen. I remember my mom going downstairs and then coming back upstairs to take us out of the bathtub. I remember walking out of the room and seeing a bruise on her arm. It's such a hard memory to have.

My mom and dad are back together now. He's apologized so many times since then for the pain he caused our family. I just can't imagine going through a total divorce. It was hard enough — the separation and the fighting — at that age. I'm just so thankful that it didn't lead to a divorce.

Toben: How long were they separated?

Michelle: I think they were separated for about a year. He was actually living with another woman. They were going to get a divorce — there were divorce proceedings. But the judge wasn't going to give custody of the kids to my dad and he really wanted full custody. The whole time, my mom contested the divorce. She said that she still loved him, that she believed marriage was meant to last forever, and that's what God wanted her to do. My dad told her, "I don't love you. I don't want to be with you anymore." His girlfriend came over and said, "Stop contesting the divorce; we want to be together." Mom hung on through everything. When he couldn't get custody, it got dismissed. But he still lived in his apartment after that.

Eventually he moved back into the house and I remember him sleeping in the study. I remember he would leave weird, nasty notes for my mom that would make her cry. I can't believe my mom hung on for so long. It was such a long process — all through elementary school. From the study, back into the bedroom, back into a relationship where he loved her. I don't know if I could ever do what my mom did, but I admire her so much for holding our family together. I can't imagine the pain. I remember her getting up some nights from dinner and going into the living room to cry.

I was so confused. I loved both my parents. One of my favorite things to do when I was young was to go to the library on Saturdays. They'd show little movies and then you'd get to read and check out books. My dad would take us to do that. I remember coming back one Saturday feeling really guilty about having such a good time with my dad because my mom was in such distress. I didn't understand.

Toben: How does that affect you now?

Michelle: I know you could never say, "I would never cheat on my spouse or do anything to hurt my spouse" — but I think I have a stronger commitment to marriage because of all that happened. I can honestly say that I don't think I could ever do anything to hurt Steve intentionally. I just don't think I have it in me. My mom's devotion to her family and to God has taught me that sometimes you have to do the hardest thing — even though conventional wisdom would fly in your face. I can remember saying to my mom in high school, "Why didn't you just leave him?" She went against everything that anyone would tell her to do and stuck with her husband. And it paid off for her. They have a great relationship now. I think I would have been a totally different person if my parents had divorced. I'm so thankful for her keeping the family together, because that's why I have the life I have.

Rebecca: How did they finally resolve everything?

Michelle: I don't really know. I can't point to a specific time or event. It was gradual and happened over so many years. I was so young and didn't know a lot of the things that went on. It wasn't until maybe 1992 or 1993 that Dad said, "I've apologized to your mom so many times, but I need to apologize to you kids for what I did to our family." He described it as a fit of craziness.

Robb: Were you angry with him?

Michelle: At the time, no. I don't remember being angry at him. Later on, I was angry. There were traditions that he established during the time they were separated that bothered me. He would always go skiing with his friend during spring break, which was my brother's birthday. I remember my brother being really upset one year because he really wanted Dad to be there. I remember being enraged that he couldn't postpone the ski trip to be there for my brother, Shawn.

Toben: My parents didn't get divorced—they're still together. But we had a similar dynamic because of Noelle. When she finally really flipped out, she stabbed my dad and they had to put her in the hospital because she just couldn't stay in the house. It was so confusing. Part of me was so glad that she was gone, but I also felt guilty that I was glad. Ever since I was little, she was a destructive force.

The day she went into the hospital was the day Ronald Reagan was shot. Dad was never home when I got home from school, but Mom almost always was because she worked out of the house. I remember coming home from school and both of them were gone and I didn't know exactly where they were or what was happening. I remember watching the coverage of Reagan's assassination attempt over and over, and they called and said they were checking Noelle into treatment. I wanted to know what that meant. *What does that mean for the family? Is this like overnight camp or was she coming home or what?* They came back and said she would be in there for at least a month or so.

Right after that we went on a little vacation to the mountains—just the three of us. It was incredibly restful because we didn't have to worry about her. At the same time, there were these guilt feelings because they locked her up. I remember wrestling with feeling good and then feeling bad because I felt so good about what had happened.

That was just the first in a long line of similar situations. I ended up going to therapy for a while to try and figure things out. I'd date the most screwed-up girls I could find. I mean, "suicidal chicks" were my thing for a while. I was always trying to fix these screwed-up people who would cut themselves and dabble in suicide – sit in the garage with the car running and things like that. I had to do a lot of work to get through those things. But it felt like a divorce – a separation in the family.

Q: My family wasn't very structured either, but it was more from a philosophical standpoint. They went to great strides not to put any preconceived notion into us as kids. They were very open to discussion. "We want to help you make the right decision for you." "We want to help you understand who and what you want to be." But at the same time, it didn't provide the kind of structure where a twelve-year-old could make those kinds of decisions. I think they had very good motives and were trying to do what they felt was right. But I don't think they provided what they thought they were providing.

Our family became a foster family for about five years and we had about twenty or so babies during that time. And that provided an extreme amount of structure. The family unit functioned very well like that. It was a relief when we had a baby because everyone knew what they had to do. We were all assigned different tasks and everyone was focused because it was all about providing for this helpless infant.

Even now, my parents offer advice in a non-advice sort of way. When I ask their opinion, I want them to tell me what they would do in a particular situation. But I usually get their ten top answers and then I have to figure it out myself. In some ways that's good, but in some ways it's frustrating because I'm never sure if I'm heading in the right direction.

I think my family is garishly normal – totally, utterly normal. Values were definitely given to us as kids. I grew up going to church. My grandfather was a pastor; my mother and father both worked in the church. Christian values were enforced – the right behavior. But as far as their expectations – "We want you to grow up to be a doctor" – they were very, "Whatever you decide you want to do with your life is fine with us. If you want to be a garbage collector, we want you to enjoy that to the best of your ability and we'll support you." I remember as I got older I became almost resentful that they didn't give me more suggestions. It didn't help me to not have direction.

Joanne: My family was totally different. We were very structured. Everything from the rules about how you behave when people come over to when you go to bed to what you wear when you go to church to what you wear when you go to school.

It's different now. In my family there was definitely a right way and a wrong way to do things. As a young child, that was good. It felt very safe to me. But as I grew older, I felt trapped by it. And that caused problems. I can honestly say that my parents have changed a lot. Now that I'm on my own and independent, I think the difference in our families, Quentin, is that if I were to go to my parents now and say, "Here are my options and I don't know what to do; what would you do if you were me?" I think they would tell me.

Robb: You're pregnant now. How would you raise your child differently?

Toben: That will be complicated. Because it's our child—Joanne's and mine—and our upbringings were so different.

Joanne: I want to treat early childhood the way my family did. For example, I want our children to have a bedtime. I think bedtime is good. If a kid is in bed by 8:00, that gives me downtime—alone with Toben. Time that I need. Time to review the day, to talk about things that aren't appropriate to talk about in front of kids. I'm not as concerned about a lot of rules—"Don't jump on the bed!" I think jumping on the bed is kind of fun every once in a while. The kinds of structure I like are manners at the table.

I think the thing that I'd do like Toben's family is to offer more areas of responsibility as kids grow up. I'm not going to say what time you have to be home, but I want you to tell me what time you're going to be home. And because you said it, you'd better be home by that time. As kids get older, let's major on the majors; give kids the opportunity to make some important choices and the opportunity to fail while they're still at home and there's still that safety net. I think that's something Toben's family did really well. In my family, I wasn't allowed to do that as I got older. I had to be good all the time. Failure wasn't an option. We had to keep up appearances. But my early childhood is full of great memories. I'd love for our child to have those same kinds of experiences.

Toben: I'd agree with all that. I definitely want our children to have that sense of calm and peace and structure and normalcy and all those things that I sense Joanne had as a young child. But I think my tendency will be to parent the way I was parented.

My little sister, Faith, is Noelle's daughter. She came out of an abusive situation, so my parents' biggest focus is to make her feel loved and important. If that means she wants to run around the house like a maniac, that's probably okay most of the time. My mom told me once that a lot of the things they did as parents were born out of convenience. I think they're trying to be very conscious of when Faith wants to do something that's obnoxious—my mom's first thought is to decide if it's bad or just inconvenient.

Robb: That must be interesting for your parents. How many times do our parents have a second chance to parent? It's so rare for them to actually get to do things differently instead of just looking back twenty years and saying, "I think I'd do that differently."

Joanne: But if you have younger brothers and sisters, did you notice a difference in how they parented just in that short period of time?

Steve: I'm the youngest of seven. The difference in treatment was huge. My brothers and sisters would tell me all the time that there's no way they would have gotten away with the stuff I did. It made me feel good for the most part. The bad thing was that I got all the hand-me-down clothes. I have three older brothers, so my jeans always had more patches on them than anyone else's. I very rarely got new stuff. But by the time my mom got to the seventh one, her parenting was much more relaxed. "Oops! I stabbed the kid with a diaper pin, but at least I didn't stab him the three previous times I changed him!" My older brothers and sisters paved the way for my insolence.

Rebecca: The youngest gets away with everything—anything and everything she wants to do!

Sarah: Our youngest sister is unbelievable. She even talks about it: "I have Mom and Dad wrapped around my little finger!"

Rebecca: Sarah and I grew up together. There's a lot less of an age difference between us. When Hannah was born she was like a second part of the children. She talks about that all the time too.

Sarah: Hannah's four years younger than Rebecca and six years younger than I am.

Rebecca: Sarah and I are only two years apart, so we went to school together and we had a lot of the same friends. We got away with the same things together. With Hannah, she got everything she wanted and she still does!

Toben: That's so funny because I had almost that same thing, but I was the oldest, so it was flipped. Noelle's behavior was so bad that she paved the way for me even though she was two years younger. I did a bunch of stuff that would have seemed like a big deal if she hadn't been there. I pierced my ear with a safety pin, in my bathroom. And that was so much less extreme than the stuff she was doing that it probably seemed like no big deal to Mom and Dad.

Rebecca: That's like you too, Robb. Your brothers did stuff. . . .

Robb: We had four kids in our family and I have two older brothers. It was like we had two families—one with six of us, and one with only four of us. My sister would probably say that there's a third family—just her, Mom, and Dad.

My brothers paved the way. I was so observant. I went through growing up as the stable, never-does-anything-wrong one. I just didn't draw a lot of attention to myself. My two older brothers were always in trouble, and my sister was the only girl. I was just always kind of there. My parents would come and ask me, "How are you doing?" If I did things wrong, I thought about them more. I thought about the consequences because I saw what my brothers were doing wrong. I made decisions a lot better. If I really wanted to do something and knew it was wrong, I thought about it carefully and did it.

Toben: That's so strange. Most people don't think about the consequences. It's not a calculated risk for them. I was the same way though. I thought, "If I smoke, and my parents smell the smoke, what's the worst thing that could happen?" And if the consequences weren't that bad, I'd go for it.

Rebecca: I never did anything wrong. And that's not an exaggeration.

Sarah: It really isn't! I was so good about lying about what I'd done and Rebecca was so quiet.

Rebecca: I spent a lot of time by myself in my room and was really quiet. My parents would always think I was doing something wrong, and I really wasn't.

Sarah: I was the golden child—even though I was running around doing the worst stuff.

Rebecca: I got grounded once for going to the mall instead of going to youth group. But I didn't go to the mall *instead* of youth group; I went to youth group *late*. But I got grounded. And that's like the worst thing I ever did. Sarah and I would joke about it, because Mom and Dad really had no idea that I was so good and Sarah was so bad.

Robb: Do you really think they had no idea? Not even your dad smelling alcohol on Sarah's breath? Do you really think they were oblivious?

Sarah: Not oblivious, no. I think they just didn't want to deal with it. When I was acting out so much and would go out and do all these things, they didn't really say anything. At one point, my mother thought I was going down the path of depression, but she never talked to me about it until afterward. Much later she said, "That whole time, I was so afraid for you." I was like, "Why didn't you say anything?" All of a sudden, one day she's bawling—but it was years later. I was so into being an outcast—I'd wear jeans with holes, weird earrings, white tee shirts, black high tops.

Rebecca: You really wanted to be an outcast, but you weren't!

Toben: I started shopping at Goodwill and I would buy XXL flannel shirts and anything with holes in it, and I'd write on everything—with black marker. I'd get my hair shaved except my bangs—they'd be really long. My parents were so cool about it. I could dress like that to church if I wanted. They just didn't sweat it because of everything else that was going on. I think they thought, "If the worst thing he does is dress funny. . . ."
I thought I was so cool! You look back and see those pictures—ugh! That must have been really hard for them.

I see kids in our neighborhood and think that if I were their parent, I'd never let my child dress like that. And then I remember that my parents were cool about that.

Steve: I had to wear dress shoes to school.

Toben: Because of your school or because your mom made you?

Steve: Mom made us. All the time. They didn't wear out as fast as tennis shoes. It wasn't until about sixth grade that I could wear whatever shoes I wanted. My brothers and I climbed trees all the time. And since trees wear shoes out, Mom got us the shoes with the stiffest leather she could find.

Robb: So you climbed trees in dress shoes?

Steve: That's all we had!

Sarah: What? Like little wingtips? I just get this picture of you climbing trees in wingtips!

Steve: We didn't have money to replace shoes all the time. I grew up completely without a dad. He died when I was three months old. My oldest sister was eleven. My mom raised seven kids by herself. Never got remarried. She was home and didn't have to work because of Air Force benefits of some kind.

Q: What was that like? All your older siblings knew your dad and you didn't.

Steve: It got more annoying as I got older. I hoard as much of his stuff as I can when I find it. I still look for his stuff when I go home now. I wear his class ring. I have his coin collections. I hoard his stuff because I didn't know him. I figure having his stuff is my compensation for not knowing him.

I did a lot of bad things when I was growing up, I guess. I got away with it because of my brothers and sisters. Some stuff Mom talked to me about and some stuff she didn't. And then, I remember as a senior in high school, she looked at me one day and said, "I know a lot more about what you do than you think I do." Uh oh.

Toben: I think my parents knew, but they never said anything.

Sarah: Everything?

Steve: My mom would know stuff that there was no possible way for her to know. I could do something with no one else there and she'd know. She said God told her, when I'd ask her how she knew. And since it was my mom, I didn't argue. "Okay, God told you and I get in trouble."

Sarah: Thanks, God!

Steve: She always said that she'd ask God that if she wasn't there to see me do something wrong, someone else would see me and tell her. You do something at school, and Mom knew about it. You'd go home and Mom would say, "So you had to punch him, huh?" You'd deny it, but she'd always say, "That's not what I heard."

Robb: It's that grapevine. It was the same way for me. My mom knew everything. She was the director of the grapevine and she knew absolutely everything. "So I heard these parents are out of town this weekend and you were out last night until midnight. Where were you?" It killed me.

"Mistakes"

Mistakes are rarely fun. They can be costly, embarrassing, and painful.
But acknowledging the mistakes we've made in the past and learning from them
helps make the present and future a little more bearable.
What's a mistake you made in the past? What have you learned from it?

"Firsts"

Go back to the list of firsts at the beginning of this section.
Pick a first and tell a story about it.

"The Wonder Years"

What was growing up like for you? What kind of things do you remember?
Are there things you really liked about your family? What would you change?

PART TWO

WHERE I AM

STORIES ABOUT THE PRESENT

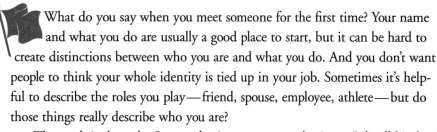

What do you say when you meet someone for the first time? Your name and what you do are usually a good place to start, but it can be hard to create distinctions between who you are and what you do. And you don't want people to think your whole identity is tied up in your job. Sometimes it's helpful to describe the roles you play—friend, spouse, employee, athlete—but do those things really describe who you are?

The truth is that who I am today is a pretty complex issue. I do all kinds of external things either because I have to or because I love to. Then there are those internal things too—where I'm growing and the struggles I'm still trying to work out.

It's usually easier to tell people about the outside stuff—after all, those things are pretty visible. But I've found that talking about those internal issues and getting them out in the open is what makes change and growth happen. It's too easy to keep those things inside and pretend they don't exist. Learning to tell the stories around those issues is painful, but the change that comes from that disclosure is worth it.

I (Toben) have a good friend who for a long time struggled with her body image. Most of the time she wasn't comfortable with the way she looked. Frequently, I'd get frustrated with her for bad-mouthing herself. I thought, *Get over it! You're a healthy, beautiful person. Are you saying all these things just to get a compliment?*

I didn't find out until later that she'd struggled with anorexia during high

pres·ent \ prëz´ənt\ n

1: now existing or in

progress 2: being in

view or at hand

school. Her parents would send her incredibly conflicting messages about her body and eating habits. They'd tell her she was "getting a little heavy" and then turn around and scold her for picking at her food when the family ate dinner together. She'd drop a lot of weight and her parents would make comments about how she was too thin. As a result, she carried that baggage around for a long time.

The things that she said about herself made a lot more sense to me after I knew what was behind them. Over time, I was able to help her get beyond some of those body image issues, but only because she trusted me enough to let me know what was really going on. Where I wouldn't normally have had the patience to continue to boost her self-image or give her the positive reinforcement she needed, knowing what she'd been through gave me the resolve to do just that.

When we take the risk and let our friends know what's really going on with us, we'll often get the support and encouragement we need to work on the things that we feel need fixing.

Movie
Book
Song
Car
Band
Color
Place
Person
TV show
Clothing
Food
Musical instrument
Restaurant
Drink
Pizza topping
Store
Sport
Artist
Shoes
Flower
Scent
Season
Ice cream flavor
Holiday
Word
Gift
Game
Snack
Sports team
Actor
Sandwich
Meal
Poem
Vacation
Dessert
Writer
Play

These are a few of my favorite things . . .

"Raindrops on roses, whiskers on kittens . . . " It's easy to make a list of our favorite things. And they do reveal something of who we are. (Have you noticed that *The Sound of Music* is one of my (Joanne's) favorite movies?) But why is something a "favorite"? What makes it different from something you just like a lot?

I may like the ocean, but what makes it my favorite place to visit? Is it the sounds, the smells, the feeling of eternity I get from being there, or something more? Is it because being there conjures up fond memories?

Think about some of your favorite things. What has made them your favorites? Is there a story behind why they rank so highly with you?

Movie	Drink	Game
Book	Pizza topping	Snack
Song	Store	Sports team
Car	Sport	Actor
Band	Artist	Sandwich
Color	Shoes	Meal
Place	Flower	Poem
Person	Scent	Vacation
TV show	Season	Dessert
Clothing	Ice cream flavor	Writer
Food	Holiday	Play
Musical instrument	Word	
Restaurant	Gift	

"These Little Lies of Mine"

by Toben Heim

When I'm on a business trip, in an airport somewhere—well-dressed with my briefcase and notebook computer in tow—I want to run into someone I went to high school with. I want to run into one of the popular kids. One of the kids whose style, ease, and popularity heightened the poignancy of all my insecurity, fashion missteps, and angst-ridden teenage dramas. In quiet moments, waiting for the plane to begin boarding, I think, *Now is the perfect time!* I think about what I'd say, the names I'd drop, and the subtle hints I'd toss out to indicate what a success I have become. My cell phone rings. . . .

One soft drink company advertises its product with the slogan, "Image is nothing." Yeah, right.

I love image. I do a dumb thing some days when I leave the house to go to work; I count the number of brand-name labels I'm wearing. The higher the number the better. Hilfiger pants, Polo belt, Nordstrom shirt, Kenneth Cole shoes, Armani jacket, Coach briefcase. Six, that's a pretty good score. I hate that I do it. And if other people knew I did it, I'd be mocked to death. I shouldn't care about such stupid stuff, but I do.

Other days I put on my baggiest khakis and my clunky black Adidas. I wear my pager hanging from my pocket. I wear my Tommy T-shirt and my hooded Adidas jacket. I call it the "junior Mafia" look. Sometimes I wear this get-up to the office on Fridays or when I know a lot of people will be gone. I make my phone calls and return E-mail and do my adult job dressed like I should be skipping classes and hanging out in front of 7-11 or at the mall.

I've been doing it since childhood. When I was very young, maybe four, my mom dressed me in Winnie-the-Pooh separates from Kmart. You remember? It was supposed to make it easy for kids to dress themselves. Match the Pooh shirt and the Pooh pants, throw on the Pooh socks, and you have an outfit. Never, under any circumstance, mix the characters. Put the Tigger pants with a Piglet shirt and you've got a fashion disaster on your hands. I told my mom shortly after starting kindergarten that I was just a little too old to be wearing Pooh. I wanted to dress myself without the aid of storybook characters. And she let me, God bless her. It led to years of heartbreak for both my parents, I'm sure.

I made attempts at image all through junior high and high school, often with disastrous results. I was preppy. I wore Topsiders and Levi's 501s, and layers of pink shirts with the collars up. I did the New Wave thing, listened to Tears for Fears, pegged my pants, wore Chuck Taylors. I went punk and got significant portions of my head shaved, wore combat boots, and bought Dead Kennedys tapes. I went all out in each one of these stages. Different wardrobe, different music, different friends—the total package.

It was my freshman year of college when things really took off. I arrived on campus knowing almost no one, and better yet, I was *known* by no one. I had a blank slate to work with. Back home, all my friends hung out at my house. They'd been in my room. They knew my parents. I could only do so much. But here, on this college campus, I could be reborn into the image of anything I wanted. And what I wanted was to be dangerous.

I was a church kid. I didn't drink, didn't smoke, didn't dance (well). I went to youth group and Bible study and Sunday school. I weighed all of about 130 pounds, soaking wet, and had never been in a real fight. I wasn't naïve, but I certainly wasn't dangerous! But now that I was a college man it was time to throw all that aside. Don't cry for me, First Presbyterian, the truth is I never loved you. Where to begin?

Beer. Up to that point, beer was *only* about image. Drinking was something the popular kids at my high school did. When I picked up my first beer I didn't drink it to numb any pain or to lose my inhibitions; I did it to be cool, I did it to gain access. And if I can be cool picking up a beer, how much cooler will I be after three or six or. . . .

Drinking served me well for quite some time after that. It was my thing, my hook, my weapon of choice. It only got better when I transferred to a Christian college my sophomore year. Drinking was just a little more dangerous there, which suited my image just fine. I liked being the guy who could go to a party and match anyone in the place drink for drink for drink. I liked having a secret refrigerator in my on-campus apartment that was always stocked.

And it served me well after I graduated from college and started working for a Christian publishing company. Now drinking was more dangerous than ever, at least the way I'd grown accustomed to doing it. I would meet friends for a beer after work, but they typically wouldn't start with a couple of tequila shots. And they wouldn't go home after that and make martinis. And they certainly wouldn't do that every day of the week.

Then, almost all of a sudden, alcohol wasn't serving me so well any more. It began to jeopardize my image more than help it. Drinking was cool, but being an alcoholic wasn't. And being a fired-and-out-of-work alcoholic would have been even less cool. So one night, after about a dozen Cape Cods and a close call with promiscuity, I decided to quit. It took me another month to actually get around to it; I dumped my last half-bottle of scotch down the sink and haven't had a drink since. I've *wanted* a drink every day.

With alcohol out of the picture, I needed a new way to keep up the image. It didn't take long for me to realize the thing I was looking for had been with me all along. It was the thing that led me to pick up those first beers. I never lied to cover up my drinking. I was proud of that. I drank to cover the lie. That's the thing.

I'd tell stories that you wouldn't believe, except you might believe them if you heard me tell them. I've always had a talent for it. And I think I've always been keenly aware that the truth, plus or minus 10 percent, could get me exactly what I wanted. If what I wanted was image, here was a chemical-free way to enhance it.

I've never been into big, "Melrose Place" type lies. The maintenance on those is a killer. But little lies, slight exaggerations, and occasional omissions of fact are my specialty. All of this allows me to present the best, most intelligent, most clever version of myself. Of course, I did all these things when I was drinking too. In fact, alcohol helped quite a bit; it took the sting out of the conscience. That may be why (now that I am sober) these stories—these lies that served me so long—have started to fail.

I'm not ready to say that it's all been bad. I like where I am today, and I don't know that I'd be here if I'd always been honest. I don't know that I'd have come this far or achieved what I have without the image-conscious spin that I put on everything. In some ways it's my ability to sling it that makes me good at what I do. If I gave it all up, the cost might be higher than what I'm prepared to pay.

But the truth is I *am* paying. All those designer clothes (shoes, briefcases, and other trappings) cost money. If you need it, you *need* it—cash or no cash. I've financed my image at 18 percent compounded annually. I can never have a glass of wine with dinner or a drink with friends. But I will *always* want one. And the relationships I have with most people, if they were to be genuine and free of pretense, would need to be restarted from scratch.

A lot of people know the me I have *created* but not the me I *am*. I have close friends. Friends I love. Friends I'm pretty sure will love me for who I am. But even with many of them I'm unable to let down the façade I've built and polished over the years. I suspect that some of my friends see through me. I don't have the energy or the will to keep it up all the time the way I used to.

I'm experimenting with honesty in a few highly selective relationships. In my marriage, for better or worse, I'm honest. Lying to my wife never works. That doesn't mean I never put a positive spin on a negative thing, but the truth comes out eventually, and over the past few years I've realized it's just easier to lead with it. She's been gracious enough to let me get to that conclusion on my own.

I'm honest in one particular friendship because I need to be accountable to someone. I can't be a better husband or stay sober or honor my desire to know God without help. And there's no accountability without honesty.

I have a lifelong friend who has the most acute crap detector in the world. He can spot me coming a mile away. And yet he's always been so accepting of the real me that dishonesty doesn't make any sense—it doesn't get me anything.

I wish I could say I'm ready to be honest in all my relationships and in everything I do. But I'm not there yet. Here's the root of the matter: I'm too afraid. I lie because I'm afraid the truth isn't good enough. I lie because I'm afraid that *I'm not good enough*, all appearances to the contrary.

I hate that and I'm stuck with it. In the words of an old preacher, "You will know the truth and it will make you flinch before it sets you free."

Have you ever felt like Toben and wanted to run into someone from your past? What do those "perfect times" look like for you?

How has your image changed over the years?

Toben describes going to college as an opportunity to be "reborn into the image of anything I wanted." Have you ever re-created yourself at a point of new beginning? What was the result?

"The truth, plus or minus 10 percent, could get me exactly what I wanted." Do you agree with that statement? Why, or why not?

Do you have relationships where you can be completely honest? How do they influence your life?

"You will know the truth and it will make you flinch before it sets you free." Have you ever experienced this? How?

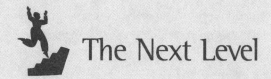 # The Next Level

What are you afraid of?

What are some of the things that make you feel secure?

Is there anyone in your life you can always count on? Who?

Where do you go to think?

Who do you admire? Why?

Do you have a mentor? Why, or why not?

What rituals do you have in place in your life right now?

What's your favorite way to spend time with friends?

Does being around other people give you energy or wear you out? How do you know?

If you could take a dream vacation, where would you go? Why? Would you take anyone with you?

How do you like to spend time with people? In a group? One on one? Why?

What do you look for in a friend?

Where do you go or what do you do when you're really angry?

What books have you read recently? What made you read them?

If you have something important to tell someone, is it easier for you to talk to them or to write it down? Why do you think that's true of you?

How would you describe the difference between loneliness and being alone?

What's something you do to relax?

If you had to describe yourself with one word, what word would you choose? Why?

Describe your ideal friendship. Is that something you're experiencing now? How?

Describe the last concert you went to.

Would you describe your life right now as stressful or peaceful? Why?

What does your ideal weekend look like?

Does your job reveal who you are to others? Why, or why not?

What's your favorite way to spend a Saturday afternoon?

When is your best time of day to get something done? Does your schedule work around that? Why, or why not?

If you could change one thing about your day-to-day life, what would it be?

Has anyone ever told you something about himself or herself that gave you real insight into why he or she acted in a certain way?

George Moore said, "The present changes so quickly that we are not aware of our life at the moment of living it." Do you tend to agree or disagree?

Samuel Johnson said, "The present is never a happy state to any being." Do you buy that? Why, or why not?

Management consultant, Edwin C. Bliss said, "Yesterday is a canceled check: Forget it. Tomorrow is a promissory note: Don't count on it. Today is ready cash: Use it!" How good are you at forgetting the past, not counting on the future, and focusing on today? Do you think this is a good way to approach life? Why, or why not?

Marie Osmond once quipped, "If you're going to be able to look back on something and laugh about it, you might as well laugh about it now." Describe a time when you've been able to laugh at yourself. How did being able to laugh about it then change the situation?

"Present-moment living, getting in touch with your 'now,' is at the heart of effective living. When you think about it, there really is no other moment you can live. Now is all there is, and the future is just another present moment to live when it arrives. One thing is certain, you cannot live it until it does appear" (Wayne Dyer). According to this statement, are you really living? What are some ways you could get in touch with your "now"?

Donald Trump said, "I try to learn from the past, but I plan for the future by focusing exclusively on the present. That's where the fun is." Do you think of the present as "where the fun is"? How does that affect your life?

Toben: Describe a formative or pivotal experience that has helped you get to where you are today.

Michelle: I'd always been in acting and the theater. Even when I was really young, my parents would put me into plays because I loved it so much and was pretty good at it.

Q: Are you acting now?

Michelle: My freshman year in high school my drama teacher told me about a play at one of the universities nearby. One of the roles was a fourteen-year-old girl. She told me they'd probably cast a university student, but encouraged me to try out for it since I was fourteen at the time. I was nervous about it. They'd had a whole week of auditions. I went the very last night and hadn't even read the script. I did the audition cold and got the part. It was probably one of the best acting experiences of my life. Three months of intense rehearsals and then a three-week run of the play. I felt great and decided this was what I wanted to do with my life. I won an award for the part.

It really became my passion and I thought about acting all the time. At the end of the play, my whole life was wrapped up in acting. But I felt God telling me that he didn't want me to be in acting anymore. It was a really hard decision to make because I knew I had the talent for it. I wasn't going to move to Hollywood or anything, but I thought about getting my degree in drama and teaching. I could have had a scholarship with drama. But I said no.

I don't think I would have met Steve if I had gone on with acting. I really think that someday it will come around again. I don't think God gives us abilities and talents to never use. I think that would be the pivotal point in my life where I chose one path over another.

Sarah: I totally relate to that. Choosing paths and wondering which path was right for me. When I was growing up, people always said, "Why do you want an English degree? How are you going to make any money with that?" So for a long time I didn't do what I wanted, and I was miserable. I was studying science and math — and I liked them both — but I didn't want to do that forever. So I went ahead and got a degree in English. And ended up working for a computer networking company doing sales—the last thing I ever thought I would be doing. Something I don't want to be doing. When I applied for jobs after college, I applied for everything I possibly could—except sales jobs. The way I got this job was that a friend of mine was working at the company and they needed to hire eight people in about a week. They didn't have any potential people to hire and were willing to hire recent graduates. I was about two weeks out of school and was doing all this temp and part-time work. I interviewed on a Wednesday and flew to training on Thursday. It was a bing-bang-bam thing. I sort of haven't looked back since.

I was married at the time and needed something to support me and my husband while he was still in school. I needed something that was going to be enough money to live on. And it ended up catapulting me into a career that is very lucrative. But it's still not what I want to be doing. I'm not invested in this—I'm not into the big-business corporate world. I want to get into something where I have more decision-making power, where I'm more invested in the product I'm selling. Or something completely different. I love to read, and writing is fun and challenging for me. So I have a job that really is great—it pays the bills and much more. And I have to do it for the foreseeable future, knowing that there's something better coming. But still, having to continue to be focused and doing well at the job I do now has been a real challenge for me.

Michelle: I feel the same thing. It's going to be soon. It's exciting, but it's scary. I relate to trying to do your job and doing it well. You can't drop the ball even though you're totally not interested in what you're doing anymore.

Sarah: I go to work every day, but if there's not very much to do or if it's not at all challenging, I feel like "Why am I bothering?"

Toben: I think a pivotal thing for me was doing student government in college. It was such a transition into success. High school was so miserable because of everything that was going on with my family. And my freshman year of college was a disaster too. The big thing was taking the risk to run for student government—I'd never done anything like that—and winning! That was just the greatest. I remember thinking, *From here on out is real life.* It was this great positive thing to start. Everything seemed so grown-up and so cool—going to meetings and interacting with board members. It taught me so much. Sometimes when people ask me what I majored in I tell them I majored in student government because that's where I learned everything I use today in what I do. My major was helpful, but the real formative experiences were those brutal student government meetings. Fights and crying and terrible stuff would happen, but it made me feel successful—like I could succeed.

Sarah: I assume it taught you too about how to listen to people's arguments. We would go round and round arguing about the stupidest things, and everyone would have to say their thing—and it was all these people saying the same thing over and over!

Q: Now he just shuts people down.

Sarah: I can relate to that. I remember when you were running for office and I was running for junior class president. Rebecca was visiting campus with a friend of hers, and they made all the posters and hung them up because I was so scared about seeing my name in all those places.

Toben: It's the first time in my life that I had to put myself on the line, totally, and convince other people that I had value or worth. And to have people affirm that felt pretty good. I don't know what would have happened if I'd lost and it had turned out the other way. I'd probably be warped.

Sarah: I lost the election the following year.

Toben: But you'd had some experiences of winning by then. And you still stayed involved.

Sarah: And that's the whole thing. When you lose things, you have to learn how to stay involved anyway—whether or not you get the big power position.

Rebecca: I remember when I ran for freshman class president. You guys had to call me and tell me that I didn't win. I just remembered that. But then, look how the guy who won turned out—winning isn't everything!

Steve: So you actually did things when you served in student government? Two guys ran at my school and their slogan was "Vote for us, we want to pad our résumés!" And they almost won. I voted for them.

Toben: No, we actually had to do stuff! How about you, Robb? What was your formative experience?

Robb: This all ties into what I'm doing now and what people wanted me to do when I was growing up. I was so stable and a really good kid. My parents always said, "You should go into business. You're good with numbers and you're always saving your money. It's a strong field and you'll be able to support a family." I really believed that and went into college wanting to be a business major. I went into my first business class and I hated it. Then I went through the years where I really didn't know what I wanted to major in, but I continued to hear that business was what I should do. I ended up majoring in psychology. And my parents supported me, but I was still getting pressure from them and wondering how I was going to support a family someday.

I got out of college and applied for a job tied to my major—working in a mental health center—and I didn't get it. So I thought maybe everyone had been right. I applied for a business and sales job. Got the job with a great salary, went to training for three weeks, came back, went to work—and I hated it. I sat there with this thing in my ear, looking at a computer screen, trying to get people to buy things they didn't want, and sometimes having to lie to get them to do it. Sales is great for some people, but for me, it just wasn't working. I needed to get back to what I wanted to do, which for me is working with people.

I get my energy from working with people, and I think that all people go through times when they need help. If I can be that support for them and help them through that, that gives me energy.

After that business job where I had a taste of that world, I did get hired on working with mentally ill adults, as a case manager. And I've been doing that ever since, and now I'm going on to get my master's degree. I honestly feel that God has put me on this road. I was able to go test some things out, and I'm glad that I was able to do that because now I know

what I *don't* want to do. I really feel like God is leading me in this direction—applying to graduate schools and not getting in the first year, applying the second year and getting into four of them. The timing just shows me that if I'm patient, God does show us where we're supposed to be. It's not always on my time. I'm not always a patient person, and that's very difficult for me. But every step of the way I know that this is right. My whole body feels that this is where I'm supposed to be. It doesn't pay a lot of money; I'm not bringing in big sales or flying all over and doing marketing—even though there's a part of me that says, "Gosh, that's what I should be doing because I'll be recognized by my friends and my family." But when it comes down to it, I love what I do every day.

That's been a real struggle for me, even going into grad school saying, "I know this is where I want to be, but I don't know if I'm completely supported by going this direction." The questions are "How are you going to raise a family? How are you going to do it?" But if God's bringing me in this direction, he'll provide those things. This year going into grad school—even though it's been difficult and challenging in so many areas—I know this is where I'm supposed to be. It's one of the first times I've had this great feeling. I love what I'm doing. I've

never had that before. And I don't know that a lot of people necessarily get that, or if they do, they don't have it for a long period of time. It's been a long, hard road, but I feel good about what I'm doing, where I'm going, and who I'm serving. I still feel like these are my gifts and I'm using them. And that's a nice place to be right now.

Joanne: You talk about using your gifts and how you do that at work. One of the things that came up when we were describing who we are was not liking our jobs. And I think Robb's right; there aren't very many people who really love their jobs. I mean, I like my job, but I could still walk away from it. For me, there are just more important things. If our gifts aren't getting used in our jobs, where are they being used? Where do we find that fulfillment?

Robb: I don't know. I think there are a lot of people whose interests and gifts don't hook up with their jobs—and that's probably pretty normal. As a person, you have to seek those opportunities out—through volunteering or whatever. It's so easy to say, "I work and I'm busy doing these things." We have to go find those things so we can have that fulfillment.

Sarah: I've really done a lot of thinking about that lately. I have a lot of friends in my industry. I've been talking about leaving my industry and doing something completely different, which would pay about less than half of what I make right now. Everyone thinks I'm crazy because I'm going to give up all the money. I've thought about that a lot: What is it that makes you happy in a job? Makes you happy in life? Feeding who I am as a person and going after those things that really make me happy have started to dominate over making a lot of money. I know money seems like a big success indicator, but it really doesn't buy you that much.

Toben: It's been radical for me to talk with you about that, Sarah, because I've always been flipped on that. I love what I do, and every day that I go to the office I'm happy to be there. And some days when I don't have to go there, I go anyway, just because I dig it. But I've always thought in the back of my mind that I'd leave it for more money. I'd go work for a company I didn't like as well, to a position that maybe didn't give me as much freedom, if I could make that kind of money. And I totally thought that . . . until we started talking, Sarah, and you'd tell me, "You're so lucky because you like what you do." And now I don't think I'd leave for more money. Now everyone has a price, and I can be bought, but I'm much more conscious now of knowing that I'm really happy every day with what I do. And maybe it's okay that I'm making less than what I could make.

Sarah: It makes a huge, huge difference if you can find things you like. I did this before in California and now I'm doing it in Texas. I'm happier in Texas because I have more friends now than I had before. I still don't meet a lot of people out there that I just click with, but at least I have more friends than I had in California. And I'm involved with things at church in the college program. I meet with students and go hang out with them on campus. And that's part of the thing that keeps me going. I tend to do a lot of things for myself to help me stay sane. I love to read and so I make it a priority to read a lot and to give myself time to do those things and to not feel compelled to spend eighty hours a week doing a job I hate. Because if I'm going to hate my job and can get my job done in forty hours a week, I'm not going to go in there and spend eighty hours a week doing something just to make myself look better, to make it seem like I'm working harder, or to get status from all this busyness. I can go in and work eighty hours a week and stare at my computer screen and generate all this documentation, but the thing is, if I don't like what I'm doing and it's not making me happy, why am I wasting my time? There are so many other things I can do, and starting to work on other things—those things keep me going—that's what gets me up in the morning.

Toben: Even though I love my job, there are areas where I've felt like I don't get to use my talent—my creativity or other things. It's been fun to say, we're going to do this deal and I don't know if anyone will want to look at it or do anything with it, but we're just going to do something creative and fun. In my job, I rarely get to see immediate results. Maybe four months later a sale will happen or we'll get a promotion, but it's not like I go to work and at the end of the day I have something that I've built that day.

Q: It's important just to realize for myself that I am not my job. I can do anything—I may love it, I may hate it—but I can do anything. It doesn't affect who I am. God has gifted me in different ways and I can use that in a work situation, but if I was unemployed and didn't have a steady income, I would still be who I am and still use those gifts. That comes out of my upbringing—my parents enforcing the idea of being who you are. "Do what you like to do if you can do it. But if not, still be you." In one year I had three major moves—Colorado Springs, Seattle, Kansas City, Colorado Springs—and three major job changes with variances in income. I was trying to cope every day with what was going to happen the next day. It was a lot of fun, but at the same time, very nerve-racking, very scary, very whatever. It wasn't a fun time, but it was one of the most fun times of my life. I could look outside the picture and look in and see that it's true—I'm not my job, I'm not an income, I'm not a paycheck. I am who I am. That's been really good.

Working with my church is probably more of who I am than my job is. I do love my job—the company and what I do there and the product we sell. Even with those positives, more of who I am is what I do at church. I've always been involved with kids somehow. I love working with them—I find it fulfilling.

Joanne: What's your greatest fear? What are the things you struggle with?

Sarah: My greatest fear is growing old alone.

Joanne: The thing that I struggle with is feeling like I have to have it all together all the time. Like it's not okay for people to come over if the bathroom's not clean. It's more than appearance, it's feeling like emotionally I have to have it all together. I have to always respond in a mature fashion. It's feeling bad when I fly off the handle, when you know what? I'm human and I have emotions and they get the best of me and sometimes that's just what happens. It's this feeling that I have to be perfect all the time. That manifests itself in all different ways.

Sarah: I'd imagine feeling the need to be perfect would manifest itself even more as a parent.

Joanne: Yeah, it's feeling like I've got to have it together all the time because if I don't, what does that say about me?

Toben: I struggle with the fact that I so rarely feel in the moment. I feel like I'm never where I'm at—I'm always looking forward to something. Like with the baby, it was all about all these steps. You get the ultrasound and find out the sex of the baby, then you move the office and set up the nursery. I had this constant "to do" list that's a year long. When the baby comes, Joanne's job transitions, which means having to redo the budget, which means some spending pattern changes, and that will affect this thing and that thing. And it never just feels like I'm right here, right now. For a change, I don't want to think about tomorrow, I don't want to think about what happened yesterday, I just want to be in the moment.

Joanne: That's a hard thing to do. When I'm at work I'm thinking about what needs to be done there, but I also find myself thinking about what needs to be done at home when I get home tonight.

Robb: We're very future-oriented. I don't think many people live in the moment anymore. It's the way our society is going. Everything is looking ahead and making sure that you have everything in place so that by the time you get there, you're okay.

Joanne: That's good up to a certain point. I think we need to be responsible and plan for things that happen in the future. But if that obsession with being responsible and having everything planned down to the perfect detail for the future is all that makes up our present, then that's *all* we have. That's one of the things I love about the friendships we have right now. I love that we can go away to the mountains—there's no television, and we can all just hang out in this house. You just *are*, you can just *be*. You get up when you get up, you stay in your pajamas all day. It feels like life should be like this. Whatever I'm doing I should just be paying attention to how it feels and not dismissing it and thinking, *This is nice, but there's this thing over here I've got to start worrying about.*

Toben: I'm starting to be afraid of what I'm missing by doing that. I'm starting to wonder, "*What didn't I experience today or take advantage of because I was thinking about this next deal?*"

Michelle: Sort of related, I struggle with not having enough time. And feeling like I'm so young, but my life is slipping away so quickly.

Toben: Exactly. And like you've got to get stuff done before you get much older.

Sarah: And then it's all over.

Michelle: There's no time to have fun, there's no time to relax, to pursue my abilities or my gifts.

Toben: You just want to be a slacker!

Michelle: I do.

Toben: Go to the coffee shop . . .

Michelle: Yeah!

Sarah: I need six months of being a slacker!

Rebecca: Wouldn't it be nice if you could figure out a way to get paid for that?

Joanne: That's such a stereotype of Gen X, "You're just a bunch of slackers." But my response is, "You don't know me at all if you think I am, but gosh! I would love to live down to your expectations!"

Robb: Yeah, let me try!

Joanne: Let me move back in with my parents and have them take care of me. I'd love to work at Starbucks or read books at Barnes & Noble all day!

Michelle: There are so many expectations—especially in my field—that you put in really outrageous hours. I just got to a point where I know I could do this: I could work eighty hours a week, and keep doing this—less time with my husband, have a family but not spend any time with them. But that isn't what I want at all. I have those issues of wanting to be recognized. I passed the CPA exam and I've done so well at this, so I should be doing this, but that's not what I see for myself for the rest of my life. That's just not what I want to do.

Joanne: If I could just hang out with my friends all day, I'd just love that.

Sarah: I have a friend who does what you do,

Michelle. He quit his job last year and went into business on his own, and he's contract-working for a couple of different places, and every Friday afternoon we blow off at 4:00 and go see a movie. And I think those are the things I want to make a priority in my life. That I can go, "It's 4:00 on a Friday afternoon and I've put in about sixty hours this week; I don't need to work until 7:00 or 8:00 tonight — it's Friday!" Because he's running his own business, he's become such a different person where he's so much less stressed out than he used to be. And going to a movie in the middle of the afternoon is a totally open option. We send out an E-mail to everyone we know saying 4:00 movie this Friday — come and hang out with us!

Michelle: I'd love to come!

Sarah: One or two people take us up on the offer out of about twenty people, because everybody's so ruled by this time clock at their job and when they can be there and when they can't. I'm very thankful that I have a job — even though I hate it — where I have the freedom to say that I'm going to a movie at 4:00 on a Friday afternoon. I'm outta here! A part of me doesn't want to give that up.

Joanne: I want to be doing things now that I'm going to remember in the future. Am I going to look back and say, "I'm so glad I worried about this, or that I took this whole day to clean my house really well even though it was already sorta clean, instead of taking this opportunity to go and build a new friendship, or whatever"?

Sarah: Or go sit on the lawn. Or go sit at a park and read a book all day long.

Robb: Or think. Just think. That's my big thing. In college I was able to think so much — about what I believe, what I don't believe, and have discussions with friends and be challenged. And with so much going on there's just not a lot of silent time just to be and think.

Joanne: If you could have a totally ideal day, what would it be like? If you could wake up tomorrow and just have your day be exactly what you want, what you need, what you wish your present could be all about, what would it look like?

Toben: It wouldn't involve work. Unfortunately . . .

Michelle: I think mine would a little bit. If we're talking about something to do every day, I'd like to get up at 7:00, eat breakfast, read the newspaper, go exercise — I'd love to be able to exercise. Then shower at 9:00 or 10:00, because I don't have to go anywhere or do anything. I don't want to be dressed up; I'd love to wear jeans the whole day long — not have to put on pantyhose or my little business suit. I'd love to have my own business, maybe work for four or five hours a day, cook dinner, have my kids come home from school, spend time with them, have my husband come home from work (or whatever his ideal day would involve!). We have dinner—sit down and eat dinner together. We haven't done that in so long. Then clean up the kitchen, relax, read, play with my dog, go to bed and have a good night's sleep, and not be freaked out about anything that was going to happen tomorrow.

Toben: I have an unrealistic perfect day and a realistic perfect day.

Michelle: That was my realistic perfect day.

Toben: I have my fantasy perfect day where I wake up and get in my Lear jet and fly to California to play golf at Pebble Beach and then fly home and have dinner. Then I have my realistic perfect day. The way that I work . . . I have a really weird work style because I can't sit and concentrate on one thing for a long time. I just can't. But I'm locked into whatever I'm doing; I'm highly productive at that moment. So I wish I could structure my whole day around not being at work for eight hours, but maybe over a twelve-hour period where I'd be at work for about half of that.

Come in first thing in the morning because I'm really productive in the morning. Get my coffee, do my deal, and then go do something else, and then come back to the office and do some more work. And then leave for three hours in the afternoon and play golf. Then come back and finish some things up at the end of the day. I get so unpro-

ductive when I try to lock in. If I knew what I had to get accomplished, and it was completely up to me to do that however it worked best for my personality and my work style, that would be like a perfect day. And I think I would build in more time for relationships. I would want to do way more stuff with Joanne, more stuff with you guys, with our friends. Right now, work feels like my number one priority, but I'd like to get to a place where my friends and my family seem like my number one priority and then to structure my life around that.

Sarah: I love going to the office—if I have something to do. I go in, in the morning, and if I have enough to do I feel so energized when I get out of bed. In my ideal day, if I could just feel energized and looking forward to the day when I got out of bed, that would rock. And then if I could go to the office and do work. If I could write or edit, that would be very cool. Or even make phone calls and talk to customers. The weeks that I'm in my office I love setting up the weeks that I'm going to be out of the office. By the time 10:30 or 11:00 rolls around, I'm done. I have that big period in the middle of the day where I'm not very productive at all. What I usually end up doing is going out and getting lunch or doing something like that. I would love to just be able to go see a movie in the middle of the day (which I do anyway!) and then come back and do all that other stuff—catch up on E-mail, continue to call customers. I have a lot of customers on the West Coast, so sometimes I work until 6:30 or 7:00 at night. That's how I like to do it. I love to hang out with my friends. I also love to just go home at the end of the day, have something to eat, and sit and read. I think that would be great. Those types of things are what I'd want to do. I don't get to see my friends nearly as much as I'd want to. I'd also want to do fun things—playing cards, games, that is very fun to me and I don't get to do that very often at all. Like a vacation thing only.

Toben: What about you, Steve? Michelle's off making a million dollars so you can get in your Hummer . . .

Michelle: Did you hear my perfect day?

Steve: I don't know that my perfect day would involve an office of any kind. When I wasn't working for those six months, that was mind-numbing. Every once in a while I'd had a couple of weeks off, but any more than that and you don't know what to do. But the days I was in the mountains the whole day, that was perfect because I'd get up there, I'd find a point I wanted to climb to, I'd get to that point, and I'd just sit there and listen and think and pray, whatever. Those were my perfect days. Just being out there with no one else around.

Joanne: I think mine would involve being still.

I feel like there's so little time just to be still—to be calm. A lot of times I feel like if I could have that for an hour a day, I could handle anything. Even if the rest of my day wasn't ideal, just having that time to center or not having to rush.

Q: For me being single, it would be almost the opposite of that. I have too much quiet, by-myself time. I think my perfect day would be very relational, but would also include the energy to support that. Over the years I've found that my circle of friends or the number of relationships I can support has dwindled. And now it's kind of a core group of people—that's probably my biggest fear, that the number of friends will just dwindle away and I'll be a recluse somewhere. I think my perfect day would include several people and that it would include the energy to support all those relationships and to connect with everyone on a real level—not totally serious.

Toben: So your perfect day would be a series of lunches?

Sarah: Coffee in the morning, breakfast, brunch, lunch . . .

Q: Yeah! Just having fun with people in different ways—however they enjoy having fun—just being there with them and having that energy. It's too easy for me just to go home and flip on the TV or read a book by myself and not be content, but do it anyway.

72

Sarah: Being single, there's not such a built-in social structure of people you would hang out with. I think couples have all these couple groups they just hang out with.

Toben: Oh yeah, and it comes so easy! When you get married, friends just come out of the woodwork. Those relationships just automatically form. You get a letter in the mail, "Now that you're married, here's a whole group of people waiting to be friends with you!"

Sarah: You know that I know it's not like that, but it does seem that way sometimes. At least there's somebody you go home to every night. And I know that's sometimes a blessing and sometimes it's not.

Toben: Thank you for not saying curse.

Sarah: Sometimes I go home and I just wish there were some other people around that I could hang out with. Single people get sucked into this hole—this single lifestyle.

Toben: I think sometimes when you're married, you think, *If I wasn't married I could do anything I want*. And I'm not saying I'd trade my marriage for that freedom. But I could go play golf every afternoon. You don't have to check with anyone on anything, you don't have to make any arrangements, you just go and do.

Sarah: That's true.

Robb: But it probably wouldn't be as big a deal if you could do it every day. It's not something great anymore because you can do it whenever you want. Like Sarah can go read whenever she wants, but every day, seven days a week, she needs something else.

When I think of a day that I would love to have, I think of all the things I enjoy doing, like getting up and reading the newspaper and going to Starbucks. Relaxing. Then going on a trip somewhere. Leaving on a trip to fly somewhere. Some place I haven't been that I want to just go and have an adventure and look around and just see how other people live their lives. I'd love to take Rebecca on those trips. I'd love to show her the places I've been and go with her to places neither of us have been to. And when I think about how my day would end, if this could be a really long day, I think of ending it with our friends and family, having a big barbecue, or just being with everyone that we care about. Having all the family together. It would be so nice to have everyone close because my family is kind of spread out. End it that way.

Toben: If you could work some golf into that, then that's the day I want to have too.

Robb: There's room for a little bit of golf.

Toben: Okay, I'm changing my perfect day.

Sarah: Maybe you can just come along. We have such a great time too, when we all get together. It's usually an everybody-hang-out-around-the-table type thing.

"My Typical Day"

What does your typical day look like? What things take up most of your time?
Is it work, being at home, spending time with friends? As you look at your typical day,
what stands out to you? Is it that you pack your days full? Or that you seem to have
a lot of time unaccounted for that disappears all too easily?

"My Perfect Day"

If you could have a perfect day, what would it be like?
Who would you spend time with? What would you do? Where would you go?
Why would those things make it perfect? Is there any way you could incorporate
some of these "perfect" things into your life now?

"Me"

How would you describe yourself to someone you'd never met?
What would you tell him or her about your life? Your personality? The things that have
shaped who you are today? What kinds of words would you use to describe yourself?
Are they words you like? If not, what would you change about yourself if you could?

"To Be Perfectly Honest..."

Are you usually honest with people about your life?
Do you tend to underplay what's going on when people ask, or do you have an easy time telling them exactly what's going on? Why do you think that is? How can you be more honest with people around you about the things that are happening right now?

PART THREE:

WHERE I'M GOING

STORIES ABOUT THE FUTURE

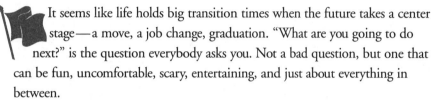

It seems like life holds big transition times when the future takes a center stage—a move, a job change, graduation. "What are you going to do next?" is the question everybody asks you. Not a bad question, but one that can be fun, uncomfortable, scary, entertaining, and just about everything in between.

I (Joanne) remember getting ready to graduate from college. "What are your plans?" was the question I dreaded. It seemed that everyone who asked it had expectations of what my answer should be, but all I could think was, *I have absolutely no idea.*

I wasn't one of the lucky ones who had a job all lined up. My last semester of college was filled with eighteen hours of course work for my two majors, spending time with friends I knew I might not see again for years, a part-time job, my marriage, and editing the college newspaper (which usually involved pulling an all-nighter once a week). There wasn't even time to send out graduation announcements, let alone seriously look for a job.

For me, the most logical answers to "What's next?" weren't the ones anyone was looking for. Somehow I knew that doing nothing for a whole day, reading a book for fun, taking a nap, or going for a long walk weren't going to get a hearty "Congratulations! That sounds wonderful" kind of response. (To be honest, that wasn't the response I was most comfortable with either. After all, there were student loans—big ones—that needed to be paid.)

fu·ture \ fyoo´chər\ *n*

1 a: time that is to come **b:** what is going to happen

79

Not knowing about the future can be uncomfortable.

But when I stop and think about it, how many of us really know that much about the future? Isn't it the not knowing that makes it possible to have hopes and dreams as well as fears and concerns?

As it turned out, not knowing what the future held after college turned out to be a good thing. Not having my next ten steps mapped out ended up opening the door for some of the unexpected things the future sometimes holds.

Not having a plan for "What's next?" meant that Toben and I were able to pack up everything we owned, put it in storage, and move to France a month after graduation. It meant having the once-in-a-lifetime opportunity to work in Paris and try all kinds of new things.

I'm not saying that it's always good not to know what's coming next. But talking and thinking about the future—telling the stories about our hopes and dreams, fears and concerns—is something worth doing. It gives us insights into ourselves and offers one more way to build relationships with others.

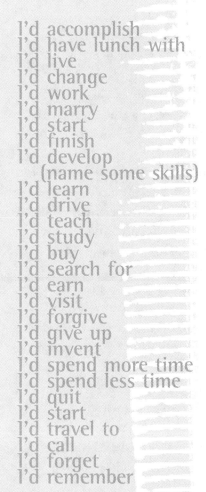

 # In my wildest dreams . . .

I (Toben) have two kinds of dreams. The first are the great, big, outrageous kind of dreams. I want to win the lottery, quit my job, and buy a house on the beach. I want to fly my friends in from all over the country to come and hang out with me. And when I travel, I want to bring my friends with me. I want to drive my daughter to school every day in my Porsche.

I have some simpler (and probably more attainable) dreams as well. I'd like to get through this week. I'd like to take a little time off and read a really good book. I'd like to get some stuff done around the house and play some golf.

It's important to be able to talk about both kinds of dreams—the great big ones and the seemingly simple ones. Here are a few sentences for you to finish. Feel free to make up a few of your own. In my wildest (or not so wild) dreams . . .

I'd accomplish	I'd learn	I'd invent
I'd have lunch with	I'd drive	I'd spend more time
I'd live	I'd teach	I'd spend less time
I'd change	I'd study	I'd quit
I'd work	I'd buy	I'd start
I'd marry	I'd search for	I'd travel to
I'd start	I'd earn	I'd call
I'd finish	I'd visit	I'd forget
I'd develop	I'd forgive	I'd remember
(name some skills)	I'd give up	

"Scheduling Life"

by Joanne Heim

I used to think about the future all the time. I never enjoyed the present because I was always looking ahead—waiting for my life to begin. And in the process, life passed me by.

There's a great quote in *Life After God* by Douglas Coupland. It's my page in the book—the page that summed up exactly how I was feeling when I read it.

> When you're young, you always feel that life hasn't yet begun—that "life" is always scheduled to begin next week, next month, next year, after the holidays—whenever. But then suddenly you're old and the scheduled life didn't arrive. You find yourself asking, "Well then, exactly what was it I was having—that interlude—the scrambly madness—all that time I had before"?

For me, the list was a little different. "Life" would begin when I moved out of my parents' house, when I went to college, when I got married, when that horrible semester was over, when I graduated, when I got a job, when we found the perfect apartment, when we got a better apartment, when I got a better job, when we bought a house, when we bought a bigger house, when . . . and on and on it went.

But every time one of those things happened, I still felt dissatisfied.

I think—no, I know—I equated "life" with happiness. And I was anything but happy. Looking to the future all the time made me bored with the present. Made me resent the present for not being the future I had hoped it would be.

Luckily, I wasn't "old" when I read that passage and recognized myself in it. At twenty-three I was older than I was at seventeen when my problems with the present made their debut. But I wasn't old-old.

I suppose my problems with my parents weren't all that uncommon. They didn't like my boyfriend. I'm not sure it was anything specific—except the fact that I loved him more than I'd loved any boyfriend up until then. Loved him enough to tell Mom and Dad that I'd go behind their back to see him if they forbade me from dating him.

I suspect now that it wasn't him they disliked so much. After all, they like him a lot now—which is good, because he's now my husband. I think what they didn't like was me. The boyfriend was just bringing to the surface all those things about me they didn't like—a fierce independence, a desire to be my own person, and the willpower to make my life my own.

As nice as it is to sit down almost ten years later and analyze what the real problem was or might have been, it wasn't fun at the time. I'd come home from dates to stony silence or, worse, yelling. I know now that they were terrified we were having sex. We weren't, but they believed—feared with everything they were—that we spent all our dates bonking each other's brains out in the back seat of his Honda. (Looking back, I'm glad to say there are no back seats in my past, just a memorable wedding night!)

After getting engaged the night before my high school graduation, I escaped to college—a place of freedom from worrying about what Mom and Dad were thinking. They were relegated to "home"—a faraway place that had little to do with professors, term papers, and cafeteria food.

Unfortunately, the newness of college wore off. But the next stop on the road to my future was trimmed with wedding bells and lace. Of course, the newness of marriage wore off too. It was supposed to make me whole and happy. It didn't. I was still plain old me—not the new, improved version I'd dreamed I'd be once the wedding band was firmly on my finger.

I'm not sure exactly what woke me up to the present. It may have been fighting about everything with my husband—from how to fold the towels in the linen closet to whether I drove too fast around corners. It could have been finding a therapist who didn't remind me of my dad, who let me muddle around in confusion without trying to gift-wrap the answers to my life and charge a fortune for them. Whatever it was, God's grace was behind it. I woke up to the joy and heartache and pain and euphoria and now-ness of the present. Without that awakening, I looked ahead to a future that might have been, and saw myself as an old, unhappy woman who progressed through her list of whens until all that was left was death.

It wasn't exactly the future I'd dreamed of.

I'll change, I thought.

Two simple words that make it sound so deceptively easy.

It wasn't.

Learning to enjoy the present meant learning to love—well, at least accept—where I was at any given moment. It meant learning to seize the day, the hour, the moment. Carpe diem. But trust me, "sucking the marrow out of life" is not as fun as all those preppy boys in *Dead Poet's Society* made it seem as they sneaked out in the middle of the night to read forbidden poetry.

Try "sucking the marrow out of life" while you clean the carpet—again— when the adorable puppy pees on the floor—again. Or when fifteen pipes burst and flood your new house in six inches of water, causing the basement ceiling to cave in the day before you're supposed to move in. Or when . . . you get the picture.

Of course, the present has its upside too. Good things have happened to me. Dealing with the present made it possible to seize "here today and gone tomorrow" opportunities like dropping everything to move to Paris for a summer job. Or to notice the little things like pinecones and aspen leaves instead of speeding by in a hurry to get "there"—wherever "there" happened to be. Those good things made getting through the bad bearable. I've learned to deal with the present and not ignore what's going on now while I wait for the future to come.

The problem with all this was that in my determination to enjoy the present, I almost stopped thinking about the future. And I don't think that's what was supposed to happen. Yes, I thought about dinner with friends tomorrow, next week's deadline at work, and the vacation coming in a few months. But I stopped dreaming.

I couldn't tell you where I wanted to be in five years, ten years, or twenty years. What my long-term hopes and dreams were. What I imagined life would be like or what I imagined *I* would be like. The future became as vague as the present used to be. It was somewhere out there, foggy and unfocused, filled with vague images that lacked detail to make them unique and recognizable.

I pushed the future further and further away. I ended up back where I began. But this time it was the future—not life—that never came. And as a result, things just happened without much planning or anticipation. I relegated the future to something I'd handle when I grew up.

But I am grown up, and my future needs some planning—and dreaming.

Sitting in the doctor's office one morning, I wondered about growing up. Most of the time, I feel like I'm about seventeen. When my birthday comes around, I stop and think about how old twenty-four or twenty-six sounded when I was seventeen. But then a few days and weeks go by, and I'm back into feeling seventeen again.

But that morning as I sat waiting for the results of a pregnancy test, I realized that I was old enough to be a mom. And that I'd been old enough to be a mom for a while. Was I really ready for this? Buying a house made me feel grown-up for a while. But a baby—a tiny person made from me and my husband who will rely on us for . . . everything? Wow!

The test was positive. I was thrilled. I was scared. I was overwhelmed. I wanted to laugh. I wanted to cry. I wanted to tell everyone I met that I—we—were going to have a *baby*. But I couldn't tell a soul. Toben was in New York on business, and I wasn't quite prepared to say, "Oh, by the way, I'm pregnant," the next time he called. Luckily we had planned for me to fly to New York and visit some friends in New Jersey for a long weekend. But I wasn't scheduled to leave for three more days.

The days dragged by as I sat in meetings, not paying attention and silently screaming at everyone in the room, "How can you just sit there and talk about work? I'm pregnant!" Wednesday finally came and I landed in New York to find Toben waiting for me at the gate. But La Guardia wasn't exactly what I'd pictured as the perfect spot to have this memory happen. We rented a car, got completely lost trying to get out of New York City, and then had to deal with a blizzard. Definitely not the right time.

By the time we got to the hotel and checked in, we were late for dinner at our friends' home. I sat through dinner, not hearing much of the conversation until Ann asked, "So when are you going to have kids?" Talk about irony.

We arrived at the hotel exhausted. We were staying at a charming inn on the Jersey shore, and our room was the entire top floor of a Victorian house. Definitely the right setting for a big memory. I handed Toben a wrapped package—binkies, pacifiers, nukkies—whatever you call them, the meaning was clear. He opened the paper, looked at me, and said "Are you . . . ?"

I burst into tears.

We stayed up half the night, exhaustion forgotten, and talked, planned, dreamed about the future. We talked about everything from names and how to rearrange the house to the kind of stroller we wanted and what we imagined being parents would be like.

Since that night, I've been thinking about the future a lot more. Mostly I wonder about what it will be like and if I'll turn into my mother. She's the greatest mom, and through it all has become a wonderful friend. Caring, warm, godly, and nurturing, she can make anyone feel at ease and welcome in her home. She can make you feel better when you're sick just by putting her hand on your forehead. She makes the best chicken noodle soup ever. And cookies? They're out of this world.

I want to be like her. But how?

When do we stop coming home from work and asking each other, "What do you want for dinner?" When do I have meals carefully planned and always have the right ingredients on hand to make them? When do we stop blitz-cleaning before company and instead have a house that is always clean? When will the ironing be done all at once, instead of digging through a mountain of clothes for the right blouse ten minutes before walking out the door? When do I have leisurely mornings with time to make breakfast and clean up before the dishes sit in the sink all day? When will I have time to make things priorities that mean a lot to me but keep getting put off?

And how will any of this happen when there's a baby around?

Part of me wonders if everything will fall magically into place and I'll become more organized and rested and actually want to clean a little every day. I hope that's how it will happen, but I doubt it will.

But it must be possible. Because when I think of my future, I think of my mother's present. How she lives now is how I want to live in my future. I want to be fully present for my daughter—to always have time for her in such a way that she never doubts that she's more important than a phone call, a pile of laundry, or work. I want to provide her with a sense of security—for home to be a place she loves to be and where she invites her friends.

I want to teach her the things my mother taught me. The value of family. The importance of hugs and kisses. That it's okay to stay home from school every once in a while when you're not really sick. How to sew. The joy of digging through junk to find a treasure at an out-of-the-way antique store. That reading can expand your world better than travel. That she can be anything she wants to be—and so can I.

I want my future to be full of taking advantage of opportunities, making memories that I'll have for the rest of my life, and building relationships that add to my life and help me grow and develop as a person. I want to focus on what's happening at any given time—to enjoy what I'm doing, who I am, and who I'm with instead of being preoccupied with other things. I want to look forward to the future and dream impossible, outrageous, and irresponsible dreams.

I want my future to be full of living the present and dreaming about tomorrow.

Do you ever feel like you're waiting for life to begin? When?

Have you had experiences you'd looked forward to not match your expectations? How did that make you feel?

Where do you want to be in five years? Ten years? Twenty years? Are you on the right path to get there?

How old do you usually feel? Why?

What do you want your future to be like?

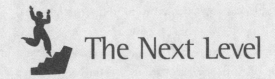

The Next Level

In his book *The Screwtape Letters* C. S. Lewis said, "The Future is something which everyone reaches at the rate of sixty minutes an hour, whatever he does, whoever he is." How do you respond to that?

What is something you'd like to do differently from your parents?

If money were no issue, what would you do? Why?

Confucius is quoted as saying, "If a man takes no thought about what is distant, he will find sorrow near at hand." Do you agree with his statement? Why, or why not? Have there been times when this has proved true in your own life? When?

What's something about the future that scares you? Why?

In the Bible, God told King Solomon he could have anything he asked for. Solomon chose wisdom. What would you ask for? Why?

Graham Greene once said, "There is always one moment in childhood when the door opens and lets the future in." What do you think he meant? Can you recall a moment when the future first became real to you?

Jules Jusserand said, "The future is not in the hands of Fate, but in ours." Is your fate in your hands or does it lie elsewhere?

Who is someone you'd like to become more like in the future? How would you do that?

Cicero said, "For my part, I think that a knowledge of the future would be a disadvantage." Why would he say something like that? Do you agree, or would you like to know what your future holds?

What is a social problem that you think will be solved in your lifetime? How will that be accomplished?

What is a social problem that you think will get worse? Why?

Do you look to the future with fear and trembling or with hope and enthusiasm? Explain your answer.

Albert Einstein once said in an interview, "I never think of the future. It comes soon enough." Do you ever feel like that?

If someone gave you the chance to look five, ten, or twenty years into your future, which one of those increments would you choose to look at? Or would you say, "Thanks, but no thanks." Why?

What did you think your future would look like when you were a child?

Do you think most people think things will be better in the future, or worse? Why?

If you could look into someone else's future—any person other than yourself—whose future would you want to take a peek at? Would you tell that person what you saw? Why, or why not?

Think about a decision you're going to have to make sometime in the future. What is it? If you had to decide on it today, which way would you go?

Seneca once said, "He is only anxious about the future to whom the present is unprofitable." What does that mean? Would you agree or disagree?

J. G. Ballard said, "I would sum up my fear about the future in one word: boring. And that's my one fear: that everything has happened; nothing exciting or new or interesting is ever going to happen again . . . the future is just going to be a vast, conforming suburb of the soul." Have you ever felt like this? What were the circumstances surrounding that time in your life? If you don't feel like this any more, what changed?

Corrie ten Boom said, "Never be afraid to trust an unknown future to a known God." Do you have that kind of confidence when you think of facing the future? Why, or why not? Does your confidence come from a known God or something else?

"That man is prudent who neither hopes nor fears anything from the uncertain events of the future" (Anatole France). Do you agree with this statement? Could you be happy if you neither hoped nor feared for the future? Why, or why not?

Toben: What will you be doing in a year?

Joanne: Changing diapers. And so will you!

Michelle: Me too, I hope. Maybe in a little more than a year, but you never know.

Rebecca: Looking for houses.

Sarah: You're going to be looking for houses in a year? In a year I want to be here, with ya'll.

Everyone: Ya'll!

Sarah: Now you're all going to make fun of my accent?

Joanne: You should hang out with my mom. She says "ya'll" all the time.

Sarah: No really, I want to be here in a year, not working at my job. And I would like to own a place as well, but . . .

Steve: I want to be in a big place with a lot of acreage, raising Ridgeback dogs.

Robb: I'll be almost done with grad school, with a job in place—a well-paying job with a company car and an expense account, as a social worker—ha! No really, I'd like to have a job in place before I graduate so I don't have to worry about that. And I guess Reba and I will be looking at houses and maybe thinking about having children.

Toben: Maybe you should move here too! If I could do anything, a year from now I would want to be managing a Gen X publishing company.

Q: I think that in a year I will still be very comfortable with my current position. I would actually know what I was doing by then.

Joanne: How do you hope to develop as a person?

Toben: I hope I'm kinder. I think I'd like to be a kinder person.

Sarah: We're all waiting for that to happen!

Robb: Why do you want to be kinder?

Toben: Because I don't think I am. When I get stressed out I think I'm very unkind. I know people that are kind all the time, like you, Michelle. You are kind to everyone no matter what is going on, and I don't know how you do it. You're always nice to people. When I get tense I'm mean to everyone—even the people I love. I try to make it funny so that I can be mean without hurting anyone's feelings but . . .

Robb: I think I'd like to be more accepting of people who have different views than I have. I think that's an easy thing to say, or to do on the surface, but I still harbor other feelings underneath. I want to achieve that to a point that I'm comfortable with it, so that when I'm around

other people I feel good about the way I'm treating them and thinking about them. And maybe that makes me sound like I'm an incredibly judgmental person, but I'm talking about the kind of people I work with. They can take a lot out of you and it's easy for your thoughts to turn to things like, *They don't deserve this.* It's easy to have that happen when you work with challenging people. So I'd like to be more accepting.

Toben: Especially with the kind of work that you're doing. I would be so bad at that.

Robb: And maybe that's why I see this as an area where I could improve, because I'm in that environment all the time.

Michelle: I think I would like to be more giving of my time and my energy. I feel like I'm very self-centered — not in a bad way, but I feel like I spend so much of my time focused on what's going on with my life; I'd prefer to be a person who is concerned more with what is going on with other people and their lives. I feel right now like I don't have the energy to be that way, but I'd like to.

Sarah: I'd like to be more honest. For a long time, I wasn't very honest with my friends or the people that I was in relationships with. And for the past three years I've been getting more honest and I want to keep developing that trend. I'm more willing now to tell people that they're full of crap and not worry about whether that person is going to go away and not want to ever hang out with me again. I don't put up with as much of that kind of stuff as I used to because I am more honest about that stuff. But I'd like to be more honest about the kind of person I am and what my addictions are and what my great characteristics are and about what I love to do.

Toben: I want to be more honest too. It's so easy not to be. Sometimes I feel like so many things encourage dishonesty. You were talking about going to your job, and in order to do it well you have to sling it. I totally feel like that sometimes.

Sarah: In sales that's a huge thing. You can really get stuck in the middle . . .

Toben: I lie about all kinds of dumb little stuff that you wouldn't think would matter. I used to lie about bigger stuff but now I just do it for convenience. I would love to have the patience and the energy to be honest all the time.

Q: I think that's what we all expect from other people, that kind of honesty, but it is hard to do it ourselves. It's a double standard.

Sarah: And it scares the crap out of me sometimes even now when I say, "You seem to be angry with me right now and maybe you need to express that." And then I get hit with this barrage of anger, and then I think, *Why didn't I just shut up?*

Rebecca: I would like to be more accepting of

myself so that I would have more time to think about what others are feeling—to be more accepting of myself so that I could concentrate on other things.

Joanne: I think I'd like to become more deliberate about the things I want to do. So often I do things just because they come up. I'd like to be more proactive about doing the things that I want. A big part of that is taking responsibility for my situation. I have a tendency to blame things on outside forces. I want to take control of my life and I want to realize that if I want something I have a choice about getting it. There are all kinds of things I want in my life and I push them off by saying, "I'm too busy" or "I don't have the time." But a lot of things I want for my life aren't that outrageous. They're pretty normal. I want my house to be clean. I want to get into a routine.

Toben: What scares you about your future?

Joanne: Being an adult. It scares me to be responsible for another life. Or that I'm living my life and I'm responsible for it too. I feel like I have a safety net with my friends and my parents. I know if I ever got into a bind, they'd help me. At least I think they would. It's not like when you're a kid and there's that parental safety net where if you don't take care of something Mom will take care of it for you. It's me, and if I blow it I blow it.

Toben: I am afraid my life is just going to go by me and that at the end of my life it'll be too late to do anything about it. I keep going forward and forward and don't stop often enough to really be in the moment. When I'm seventy, I'll look back on all that and I won't be able to do anything to fix it. And I'm afraid for our baby because the world seems to be so messed up. It's so different. I think that one of the things my parents had trouble with when I was a kid was perceiving how different the culture was that I was growing up in versus what they experienced when they were kids. I know they knew it was different, but I don't think they realized the extent to which things had changed. I think I have a good sense of how different things are now from when I was a kid but I know I don't realize the full extent of the changes that are happening. When our baby grows up and goes to school, who knows how different things will be by then. I think that's frightening. At the high school where Joanne and I went, it was a good school, but there are things that happen there now that never would have happened when we were there. Maybe we'll send her to boarding school in Switzerland or something.

Sarah: Crappy things happen, even in Switzerland.

Toben: Even in Switzerland? I feel lied to.

93

Sarah: Yup.

Toben: In some ways I'm afraid of turning out like my parents.

Michelle: And I am afraid of *not* turning out like mine. I would love to be like my mom.

Joanne: Me too.

Michelle: And I have a similar fear about when we have kids. I want to be able to instill good values in them. And that scares me.

Rebecca: That's what I fear—not doing something right as a parent. Especially having seen the effects of a lot of bad parenting in my field, with all the kids I come in contact with. I'm afraid that something I do will totally mess everything up.

Michelle: I would love to be like my mom. If I could have a fraction of the strength she has . . .

Toben: There are characteristics about my parents that I wish I could emulate. But there are other characteristics I don't want to emulate, but I think that is true about any couple.

Michelle: I hope that Steve and I stay as close as we are now. I think that we have a terrific relationship but I don't see a lot of other examples of that out there. I hope we can keep that going through the years—especially when we have kids—that our marriage won't become strained or suffer because of that.

Steve: From my perspective, I actually wouldn't mind being like Michelle's parents either. Had Michelle not told me about all the struggles her family faced with her parents' separation and almost getting divorced, I would never have known. When she told me I was like, "Get out!"

Michelle: And I think it's because of how hard that time was for them and that they got through it. Now sometimes they are almost like teenagers, they're so in love. They are so close and openly affectionate. That's a great example for us.

Sarah: Our parents are in their fifties. Wait. Late forties.

Rebecca: This is going in print.

Sarah: Okay. Our parents are in their late forties and they are so disgusting. They are totally like teenagers again. And we're always like, "Get a room!" But I would love to have that kind of relationship, but it took them so long. I mean, all of a sudden it's like a relief because we grew up and none of us are screwed up. So it's like they have this big sigh of relief.

Toben: Maybe they're relieved that all the kids are finally out of the house. Maybe they're relieved just to be alone.

Sarah: And that we didn't all grow up to be mass murderers.

Robb: Not yet, anyway. I think one of my fears completely has to do with family. And not so much because I don't think I'll make major mistakes, but I hope I'll do the right things. I think that we live in a society where as parents you have a lot of influence over your kids, but for the most part your kids are out there and you can only do so much. Really, the way they learn is from their friends and teachers and television. That's what concerns me. Am I going to be strong enough to teach them the values and beliefs that we have? And to stay a family. It seems like so many things work to pull families apart that you really have to work at it to stay together. Not just as parents, but as a family. I've seen couples, like my parents even, that when their kids hit junior high and high school, it can be so stressful and so much of your energy goes to your kids and it's easy to spend less and less time together as a couple. And then after the kids go to college you have to reconnect. You get squeezed so hard. I want to stay aware of all that. I want to keep things in perspective. Having kids will be totally difficult, and I think it will be rewarding too. More than anything, I want to stay healthy in my relationship with Reba.

Sarah: I'm afraid my life's not going to make a difference. Like it won't matter that I ever lived or not. I think that so many people live lives of quiet desperation. They go through life feeling like one very, very tiny cog in the big wheel that makes everything run. And it doesn't really matter who they are as individuals as long as they fulfill their functions. I don't ever want to be that person who just fulfills her function. I want to make a big splash and make a difference. I want the things that I do to impact other people in positive ways. I think that the scariest thing for me would be that I would end up doing something for ten or twenty years—like I could stay where I am right now for ten years and have no life. It would make no difference to anybody.

Rebecca: I think you've made more of a difference already than you know or than you acknowledge.

Sarah: What do you mean that I've made more of a difference?

Rebecca: Well, you've made a difference to me in a lot of ways. I wouldn't be who I am now without you. And I think about the college kids you work with and the people you had an impact on throughout college.

Toben: I'm sure it's easier for you to see that than for Sarah to see it.

Q: And I would say the same thing that Sarah said. I either wouldn't have any influence on people or I would screw someone up. Or I would influence them in a negative way, and they would end up saying someday, "My life was going really great until I met this guy named Quentin."

Robb: I think that's interesting because last time I was at church the pastor was talking about how a lot of times you have an impact on

95

a person and you never know it. It's not like we ever view another person's life from beginning to end to determine the effect we had on them. If you happen to get the credit for it, that's wonderful, but if you don't, that's okay too.

Rebecca: Like when they accept their Academy Award and they're thanking people and they thank you!

Robb: I think that's an interesting way to look at it—that we really can't know what impact we've had. But it would be great to be at the end of your life and to have people come up and tell you the way that you helped them or influenced them.

Toben: I hope that when we go to heaven our lives have all been captured on video so we can go back and watch it all. You could see all the close calls you had. And to see the big disappointments, the things that didn't work out that really turned out for the best.

Rebecca: And to be able to see how small those disappointments were in the scheme of things.

Toben: And then to see all the impact that you had on people. Both good and bad. And it strikes me that all of us are afraid of having a negative impact on people, but we really want to have a positive impact too, which means you have to at least interact with people. You can avoid screwing someone up by not doing anything, but you can't make a positive impact on someone without getting in there.

Sarah: It's a huge risk.

Rebecca: And I think sometimes we have a tendency to overestimate the amount of impact we can really have on another person.

Sarah: That's true.

Rebecca: All you can do is your best and then don't kick yourself if things don't turn out perfectly.

Sarah: I work with all these college seniors who are getting ready to go out into the world, and they're all so freaked out that they're going to do the wrong thing. Like somehow they're going to go out and get the wrong job.

Joanne: Take any job.

Sarah: Right. And somehow they're not going to do the "right" thing.

Rebecca: But we talked about that all the time in college. "How do you know you're doing the right thing?"

Sarah: And you feel like you have to get everything right your first time out, but the truth is you really don't. You can go down a path for a while and if it turns out that it's not the right path, then you can go down a different path.

Toben: Or you can just cut across a field or something. Who needs paths? What do you want to be able to say at the end of your life?

Q: I can't breathe! Do you know the Heimlich?

Joanne: You mean, what do we want our epitaph to read?

Toben: No. What do you want to be able to say for yourself? You're at your retirement home in Palm Springs, and one night you're on your back porch looking up at the stars and thinking back over your life. And you're old as dirt. And you think to yourself . . . what?

Rebecca: I'm glad I've still got bladder control.

Steve: Does it have to be something serious?

Toben: Doesn't have to be.

Michelle: There is a song that goes, "I would live my life like there's no tomorrow. For life is really like a gift we borrowed. I would have not confused these things . . . with the everlasting." I hope that I don't look back on my life and wish that I had lived that way. I hope I do live like every day is a gift — not confusing the things that really matter and the things that really don't.

Sarah: I hope I will look back and say, "What a great adventure. How fun was that."

Joanne: I want to have been faithful — in my relationships and in the things I undertake and in my relationship with God.

Rebecca: I want people to be able to say, "She was honest. And she was a good example." And I hope that people will miss me.

Sarah: I'll miss you.

Toben: You'll probably be dead first.

Sarah: Real nice.

Robb: I think I'd like to be able to look back on my life and just be content, but I'd also like to be able to say that I followed God's will the best that I knew how. And I want to feel good about the kind of person I was. We all have our ups and downs, but in general, I want to feel good about the way I related to people.

Toben: I want people to be able to say, "He helped me." Or "He made my life a little better." Or "He brought me some happiness; I remember one time when I was sad and he cheered me up." Or "I remember one time when I was broke and he helped me out." I want to be remembered as a person who was there for other people. Whatever that looks like. I don't want to be the kind of person whose actions are driven by what's convenient, but one who's driven by meeting other people's needs. I don't think I'm on that path now . . .

Robb: But you could be.

Toben: And that gives me hope. I think that would be the coolest way to be remembered. What's your fantasy future?

Michelle: I want to win an Academy Award.

Steve: I want to sit on top of a big mountain.

Joanne: I want to live by the ocean in a house that has a big front porch. I want to collect seashells and cook wonderful meals and read and write.

Rebecca: I want to have enough money that I can give a lot of it away.

Toben: I would love to just be a dad. Get the kids up. Make them breakfast. Drive them to school. Go to the golf course.

Robb: There is always golf in the fantasy future.

Toben: Then pick the kids up from school and do anything they wanted to do. Go to the zoo or the park or to a movie or back to the golf course.

Sarah: "Please, Dad, no more golf!"

Toben: I think a lot of parents could be great parents if they didn't have so much else going on. But they let all kind of things get in the way of what is one of the most important relationships they'll ever have. I'm surprised that I'm saying this because I'm totally career-driven. But if money wasn't an issue, that's what I'd be about.

Sarah: That's the whole thing. If you take money out of the picture and talk about what the fantasy is, then dreams can be so wild. I'm totally career-driven too but I'd just throw it out the window and go do whatever. I would want a rocking chair.

Q: I can make that fantasy come true.

Sarah: But I want a family too. And I want to be married to someone who would feel like he's as responsible for everything as I am, so that there was no shift of balance. He would have his stuff to do and I would have my stuff to do and we do them all together so that we can have fun. I just don't think it's worth it if we all have to struggle 90 percent of the time. I think struggle is important, but it shouldn't be 90 percent of your life.

Q: It shouldn't be a habit. I'd like to get married and have a lot of children. Maybe half of them would be adopted . . .

Toben: Every time Quentin goes into Baby Gap he tries to procreate with the staff.

Rebecca: That sounds like harassment.

Q: You have no idea.

Joanne: Q, you're going to be the greatest dad someday.

Q: I think that comes from always having so many foster kids around and being extremely comfortable with that. A bigger-than-life family would be awesome.

"My Biggest Fear"

When we talk about the future, it's hard to ignore those things we're scared of. As you think of the future, what's your biggest fear? Why does that scare you more than anything else? How likely is it that your fear would actually happen?

"The New and Improved Me"

What's an area of your life you'd like to improve—one that needs some growth? Why?
How can you work on that part of your life as you head into the future? How can
others, and the relationships you have with them, help you in this area?

"My Legacy"

When you get to the end of your life, how do you want to be remembered?
What are the things you want to have accomplished? What steps can you take now
to make sure those things happen?

PART FOUR:
WHAT I THINK
STORIES ABOUT VALUES AND OPINIONS

val˙ue \väl´yōo\ *n*
1: something (as a principle or quality) intrinsically valuable or desirable; *vt* **2:** to rate or scale in usefulness, importance, or general worth

opin˙ion \ə-pin´yən\ *n*
1: a view, judgment, or appraisal formed in the mind about a particular matter **2:** belief stronger than impression and less strong than positive knowledge

Opinions are like noses. Everybody's got one. Same with values. But have you ever stopped to think where your values and opinions came from?

Handed down from your parents, and influenced by everything from where you went to college to your friends, experiences, movies, books, magazines, where you work, the music you listen to—values and opinions are as diverse as people.

I (Joanne) think one of the main things that shape our values and opinions are our experiences. Some of the people I know who will never, ever touch alcohol have alcoholic parents. A few of the couples I know whose parents are divorced work feverishly on their marriages. And women are leaving the workforce to stay home with their kids because their own mothers weren't there for them when they got home from school.

My mom was always home when I was growing up. (In fact, she packed my lunch and was usually home when I got home from school, all the way through my senior year in high school.) I knew that she thought being home and being available was important, but I never knew why until recently.

Driving home from a day at the antique flea markets two hours from home, Mom told me more about what it was like when she was growing up. I'd always assumed that her childhood was a lot like mine—Dad worked; Mom stayed home and volunteered at school; sisters fought and made up.

Instead I learned that after World War II, both Grandma and Grandpa worked, leaving the house early in the morning and returning late at night.

Mom and my aunt Martha left for school each morning from their neighbors' home and went there after school. Because they weren't at their own house, they weren't allowed to have friends over after school. They ate dinner with the neighbors, did their homework there, and went home only in time to see their parents for a little while and go to bed.

Mom explained how those things in her own childhood made it so important for her to be home when my sister and I were growing up. Unlike her own mother, my mom made us breakfast every morning and packed our lunches, often leaving happy notes on the napkins. She volunteered in our classrooms, reading books out loud and helping the teacher. She made special desserts and brought them to school to share with our classmates on our birthdays. And she was always home in case we got sick in the middle of the day.

People's values make more sense when you listen to them talk about how their values and opinions were shaped. Some opinions change easily—a new ice cream flavor comes out, quickly replacing another as my favorite. But others aren't so easily changed and can be the cause of major disagreements. As we share our values and opinions with others, telling the stories around them is one way we can influence others and find common understanding on difficult issues.

If you ask me . . .

Opinions cover all kinds of things. From the best brand of ice cream to the person you vote for, each of us has an opinion. Those opinions are often shaped by our experience and can be cause for casual discussions or knock-down, drag-out fights. As you look at the following list, how would you define these words? Are your definitions shaped by your experiences or something else?

Politicians	Love	Materialism
Government	Education	Peace
Racism	Socialism	Capitalism
Diversity	Euthanasia	Rules
Tolerance	Atheism	Integrity
Abortion	Relativism	Pollution
Welfare	Absolutes	Business
America	Choice	Respect
Religion	The world	Environment
Work	Rights	Politics
Responsibility	God	War
Freedom	Friendship	Communism
Truth	Family	Morality
Success	Humanity	

"Why I'm Not So Perfect
(A Slice from Inside Myself)"

by Mitch VanderVorst

When I was asked to write my story, at first I didn't know what to write about, what would be interesting, what people would care about. I wasn't quite sure how to tell a story about my values and ideas and at the same time make it personal and narrative. I tried a couple of different things, and nothing really worked. Then one night, after a long and dragged-out confrontation with my wife, I sat down and began spilling my frustrations on the page to my friend Jim. I clicked send on the E-mail and it was off. I knew right then what I was going to write about.

For the next couple of months I tried writing again. I tried telling my story and explaining a little bit of what it is like to be me, and at the same time I tried to get in a little bit about what I think and what I value. After a couple of tries I thought I was done, and I was very happy not to have to visit it again. But it wasn't finished yet.

The original E-mail that I sent to Jim was always the benchmark. I wasn't being as honest, I wasn't as real, I wasn't as strong as what I had written in that E-mail. So I'm going to tell my story by letting you see a true slice of my life, raw and uncensored. What I'm hoping is that you can see what I think and what I value hiding somewhere in the words. Mostly I hope you see the value I place on friendship, honesty, and grace. But I'm sure you can find even more if you look.

```
From - Mon Apr 06 22:26:09 1998
Message-ID: <3529B8F1.3726>
Date: Mon, 06 Apr 1998 22:26:09 -0700
From: Mitch Vander Vorst
X-Mailer: Mozilla 3.0C-nnie30 (Win16; U)
MIME-Version: 1.0
To: Jim Hancock
Subject: Why I'm not so perfect (a slice from inside myself)
References: <8129be3e.352953b5@aol.com>
Content-Type: text/plain; charset=us-ascii
Content-Transfer-Encoding: 7bit
X-Mozilla-Status: 0001
Content-Length: 7676
```

Jim:

Even as I'm sitting here in front of the computer, I'm ambivalent. There have been many times that I've had the opportunity to say things to you, and I haven't. And many times I've thought that you've seen right through me and I've just lowered my eyes. So here we go, for what it's worth, and more for me than you.

For many years now I've struggled with pornography. One of my primary excuses is that I was exposed to it very early in my life. From before junior high I had a friend whose mother would constantly buy magazines and rent movies for us to watch. I will not guess at her motivation.

In any case, it became a habit, way before I could understand it or was even sexually motivated by it. It started off as curiosity. But then again, those are mostly just excuses.

I was "using" in junior high. I was "using" in high school. I was "using" in college. I was "using" after college. It didn't much matter whether I was dating someone, whether I had any other sexual escape, or anything else. Pretty much as long as I can remember, it has been a dark part of who I am.

There have been a couple of people in my past both in college and after that I've related this to. And they were both people who either found out I had a similar problem, or who related to me a similar problem of their own. The problem was, there was still no accountability, probably because we all still wanted to continue, or at least keep the options open.

There have been so many times when I've taken that car ride, the whole way fighting myself but knowing I was going to give in. So many looks behind my back to make sure no one was watching. So many long drives out of town and to out-of-the-way video stores or magazine stands. But most of the time I've just blatantly gone down to "my" corner store and no one ever found out.

I wish I could say I've conquered it. But will I ever? I have told Christina, but until recently it has always been something I did struggle with—-in the past.

And I can't even say that I asked for help, or revealed anything. It was pretty much found out. And I knew that it would be, and sometimes I would even leave something lying around saying, "Oh, well. If she finds it then at least it's out in the open."

With more independence, my own house, pay-per-view, and the Internet, pornography has been even more available to me. I will fight for weeks or months at a time, and then with one stray thought, I'm in the car and "let destiny run its course."

With Christina's pain and questions I've begun to cut away the excuses and try to understand why—-but still I tend to sluff off the questions, and hold on to it inside of myself. That way, I don't have to give it up completely. I have even wondered to myself if it wouldn't be better not to be married, because then I could indulge myself without affecting someone else.

Even when confronted I have lied to her to keep some part of it still my own. I have tried to figure out how much she knows, before I begin revealing. And I only reveal what she already knows. Then a month down the road, when something else reveals itself, I will admit it again, admit the lie, but still hold what is left unre-vealed to myself. And each time she seems to trust me.

And even still, I haven't told all. I have still kept some of it to be mine. I haven't been willing to let it go completely.

And very briefly in talking with her, I feel some emotion. And even writing you and being as honest as I am able, I feel only a little emotion. It's something so deep inside of me that I no longer understand it—-if I ever did. I no longer know why, or can even guess at it. It seems it is just a part of me—-of who I am, my identity. It has fed my guilt and inferiority until I no longer know if I can live without it, or if I even want to.

Yet, I do want to. I want to tear it out by the roots and be free. But I'm having a hard time getting into it. Trying to understand why and when. It's almost as if it has a life of its own, and as part of its self-preservation, it stays on the surface, not allow-ing me to get to my emotions. Keeping distance from me. And hoping that like so many times before I will just gloss over it and say that it's a struggle and I'm trying. But trying presumes failure, and I will fail again, and can see no other way but failing. And hey, failing isn't so bad. Actually that's really what I want.

I have tried to understand even without my emotions. It is my way of dealing with feeling lonely. Or at least it seems that way. But other times it is just a thought, and then an action. Partially I am sure I use it to numb myself—from many different things (loneliness, stress, guilt, pain, feeling cheated or on the short end, or like I'm not appreciated or getting my due). And then it almost justifies itself through the guilt afterward. If I am feeling lonely, I feel like crap afterward, and then I deserve to be lonely. Guilty, I then deserve to feel guilty, and so on in a nice circle.

So the question is: What's different now? I don't know. I'm trying. And even that seems so shallow of a response. I've been trying for twenty years. But I have a wife now who struggles with feeling bad about herself (and this certainly doesn't help, even though I say it has nothing to do with sex—which is probably just another cop-out). And the pain I see in her eyes and the struggles she has trusting me and believing in me and watching me turn things back on her cuts to my heart deeper than I can explain. So there is more guilt adding to the circle.

I'm really tired of it. But I don't know what to do. I don't know what will make a difference. And the next time I know she'll be home late, or is asleep in the other room, what will make the difference? I've started to feel like telling her when those feelings begin to come upon me. I haven't yet, but the impulse is beginning to come. Maybe that will make a difference.

But still I hold on so tight.

I've prayed so many times for help, even when I didn't really want it. But I can't say that it has been any help. I'm embarrassed. I'm guilty. And I know that someday I'll have to write about it. But still, telling the world is less a problem than telling my wife the truth. How can that be?

I measure "better" in small increments. Failure every day, failure every week, two weeks, a month, two months. But it's still failure. And how far away is that next car ride, that next Internet search? And who am I really kidding? Certainly not myself, but maybe myself most of all.

There has been some emotion that has broken through in writing this. But mostly when talking about Christina's pain, or my frustration at going through this over and over again. The majority of my emotion still lurks so deep inside. It doesn't want to come out.

I am not asking anything from you, and you don't even need to reply. It is just me coming clean with you, and to whatever extent with myself. And there is just so much more to write, but I really can't get there right now.

Yet, I know there is still grace somewhere.

Now, a couple of months later, I wish I could tell you how great I am and that everything—including me—is perfect. I wish I could flaunt my victory. But I can't. And if I did, you'd know immediately that life isn't that easy and happy endings have a "be kind, rewind" sticker on them.

But what about happy beginnings? I can tell you that writing my confession to Jim was an important step in my recovery. I can tell you that my wife now knows the *whole* story. And I can tell you that I wake up every morning needing God's grace just as much as the day before. And yes, there is still grace.

I'm in the process of healing and expect that it will take a lifetime. The temptations are still there, though not as strong and not as often. The biggest relief, however, is knowing that I have told my story—to Jim, to my wife, and to you. It's not a secret anymore. I don't have to hide. That has given me the strength to confront my sin, deal with my guilt and loneliness, and even find Jesus' sweet healing touch.

And that has made all the difference.

Have you ever confessed something to someone and still felt ambivalent about it?

Mitch wrote about the opportunities we have to tell our stories to other people. Do you usually take advantage of those opportunities, or do you often wait like Mitch did?

Have you ever hoped to get caught doing something you knew was wrong? When?

Do you agree that sometimes it's easier to tell the world something than to tell someone you care about?

Have you ever felt the kind of relief Mitch talks about from telling your story and no longer having to hide? Describe it.

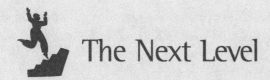 # The Next Level

How would you describe forgiveness to someone who has never heard of it?

If you could eliminate one problem in the world, what would it be? Why?

Seneca said, "Everything depends on opinion; ambition, luxury, greed, hark back to opinion. It is according to opinion that we suffer." What does that mean?

How would you define trust?

Is trust something that comes easily to you? Why, or why not?

Respond to this quote: "The only sin which we never forgive in each other is difference of opinion."—Emerson, *Society and Solitude*

What do you value most? How has it come to pass that you value that thing so much?

What opinions do you hold that seem to be unpopular with your friends?

Is there a single value or opinion that seems to be common between you and your closest friends?

Herbert Spencer, in his book *Social Statistics* states, "Opinion is ultimately determined by the feelings, and not by the intellect." What are your thoughts on his assertion?

Describe a time where you shared an opinion and felt attacked because of it. How did you respond?

Lord Chesterfield said, "A difference of opinion, though in the merest trifles, alienates little minds." What do you think he means by that?

Where do you think values come from?

How much influence did your family have on your values and opinions?

Have you ever lost anyone close to you because you disagreed strongly about something?

J. H. Shorthouse said, "All creeds and opinions are nothing but the result of chance and temperament." Do you agree or disagree? Do you think your opinions are determined by chance? Or is there more to it?

Are you uncomfortable letting people know what you really think? Why, or why not?

How open are you to other people's opinions? Is it easy for you to listen to someone that you disagree with, or do you tune the person out?

How would you define a core value? What are yours? How do they influence your life?

Thomas Jefferson said, "I never had an opinion in politics or religion which I was afraid to own." Have you ever been "afraid to own" any of your opinions? Why?

Respond to this quote: "The foolish and the dead alone never change their opinion." —J. R. Lowell, *My Study Windows: Abraham Lincoln*

How important is it to have close relationships with people who have distinctly different value systems from your own?

Can you think of a time when you have attacked someone because of that person's opinion? If you could go back, would you respond differently? How?

Irving Batcheller said, "Opinions that are well rooted should grow and change like a healthy tree." Do you agree with him? Why, or why not? Do you have opinions that don't change? Are they well rooted?

Henry Ward Beecher once stated that "private opinion is weak, but public opinion is almost omnipotent." Have you seen this proved true in your own life? Someone else's life? How?

Albert Einstein said, "Few people are capable of expressing with equanimity opinions which differ from the prejudices of their social environment. Most people are even incapable of forming such opinions." Have you ever expressed an opinion that went against the opinions of people around you? How did it feel? Or have you ever wanted to express a contrary opinion but didn't? What held you back?

"One accurate measurement is worth a thousand expert opinions" (Admiral Grace Hopper). Have you ever seen "expert opinions" proven wrong in the face of accurate facts? Describe it. How can you ensure accuracy in your own opinions?

"He who has an opinion of his own, but depends upon the opinion and taste of others, is a slave" (Klopstock). Have you ever depended on the opinions of others instead of your own? How did you feel?

Filmmaker Wim Wenders said, "The more opinions you have, the less you see." Do you agree with him? Why, or why not? Do you think that not having opinions makes you more open-minded?

Roy Disney said, "It's not hard to make decisions when you know what your values are." Describe a decision you made quickly because you knew what your values were. How would the decision-making process have been different without your values?

Samuel Johnson said that "the longer we live the more we think and the higher the value we put on friendship and tenderness towards parents and friends." Have you found this to be true in your life? How?

Gloria Steinem said, "We can tell our values by looking at our checkbook stubs." What would your checkbook reveal about your values?

What's the difference between a value and an opinion?

Joanne: It seems like friends are a huge thing. What are the things we look for in friends?

Steve: Friends are great, but seclusion to me, being way out there . . . I want to be the old hermit man sitting up on the mountain.

Rebecca: I look for honesty and for someone I can feel totally comfortable with. Someone I don't think I'll be judged by.

Toben: Two words: Low maintenance.

Sarah: Amen. I like that.

Toben: The friendships for me that have lasted the longest and have been the most rewarding are the ones where if I don't see someone every week, or if I don't call him all the time or write a letter, then he's not going to be mad. Anytime that little feeling of guilt creeps into a friendship, when I need to do all this stuff in order to stay friends, I back out. That doesn't mean you can constantly blow someone off or treat him badly or not be there for him and expect everything to go well. But some of my best friendships that have lasted for so long, it's like you might not talk to someone for a month, and then you call him and you pick back up right where you left off.

Michelle: I think a real friend is someone you can just sit with for hours, and you don't have to say anything, and that's okay.

Joanne: Yeah, that's a huge thing for me.

Toben: Bring a football game into that equation, and for a lot of guys, that is the perfect relationship.

Joanne: I love those friendships where you can spend the whole day together and maybe you only talk for two hours. Where you can sit and read a book in the same room. It's feeling comfortable, feeling safe, and totally at ease. I don't have to entertain you and you don't have to entertain me . . .

Michelle: We don't have to have anything planned out . . .

Joanne: We can just enjoy being together.

Toben: Who's responsible for that comfort? Is it that other person or is it you?

Joanne: I think it's a mutual thing.

Q: It's trusting another individual or looking for that person who you can really connect with as a friend or whatever.

Joanne: I think at some point it's a decision: "I want to have this kind of relationship with this person." And at some point you have to step out and decide, "I am going

115

to be totally me." And maybe this person isn't going to relate to that or . . .

Rebecca: I need a friend to need me as much as I need her. I need it to be an equal thing.

Joanne: And there has to be that mutual likability. Like I really, really like this person and I hope I'm not bugging her, and that she really likes me.

Rebecca: I never want to be in the situation where I'm the one always calling and the other person is like, "She always calls me and I never want to do stuff with her but I always feel like I should." So I need it to be mutual.

Toben: I think friendship should be fun too. I know a lot of people who have so many "friends" they don't have fun with. And they say, "Oh I have to go do this thing with this person because he's my friend, but I don't really like being with him." And I think that if you don't have a blast with your friends at least some of the time, then maybe you need to analyze why that is.

Q: But there are different reasons for having friendships. I may have a friendship with someone even though he's not my favorite person, but I know that I can provide something for him and he can provide something for me.

Sarah: I've changed so much in what I look for in a friendship because of the experiences that I've had with my friends. Now there's a list of things I look for. A lot of the things we've already mentioned, but one of the other things I look for is that I don't have time for somebody to be jealous of my time, so I look for people who are going to be friends with me and not have to be with me 24/7. Not to say that I'm not available to those people, but they feel like they can go out and do things with other people, and if I go do things with other people there's not this big jealousy overhanging the whole thing.

Joanne: I think back to high school where I had this one friend. I think this was mostly a high school thing, although I know this happens in adult relationships, but it was to the point where we were best friends but we didn't have any other friends but each other. I can remember when she got mono and I convinced myself and my mom that I had it too so that I could stay home while she was out of school, because I didn't want to eat lunch by myself. If she was gone, then I was all alone. "What am I going to do?" So I want both exclusive friendships and a broad range of friendships. Sometimes that's hard because I want a lot of relationships, and maybe they're not super deep but they are people I can hang out with so I'm not walking into a room with no one to talk to. But at the same time I feel like I need those few friendships that I have a lot invested in that are deep and lasting and that have a soul connection. And I think those are rare.

Toben: I think another cool thing in friendships is when you get to be with other people who bring out the best in who you are. And a part of that is accountability. Something about your personalities enhances your creative expression or your ability to think or articulate on a specific topic. Those kind of friends help you supersede who you would normally be. Sarah and I have an accountability thing going and Sarah can tell me that I'm full of crap. And it's not a big confrontational, stressful deal. It's just one person who loves another person saying, "I disagree with what you're doing."

Sarah: Honesty is a big, big issue. And I don't have all this extra time on my hands to worry about whether or not people think I'm an idiot. I want people who are going to tell me I'm an idiot. And if they don't tell me and they secretly resent me for the next twenty years—I have no sympathy for that. I'd tell them, "You chose to keep this under your hat."

Toben: Rebecca, it totally makes me wonder about those friends you were talking about earlier. If they would have taken the freedom early on to just say, "You do this thing that bugs me . . ." then you could say, "Maybe I'll change and maybe I won't." At least then you get that perspective.

Joanne: And a lot of times when you tell someone that what they do is bugging you, then it doesn't anymore.

Q: I can't imagine harboring those kinds of feeling for all that time.

Robb: I had some great friendships in college and I think I look to those as what I look for now, as far as people being genuine and honest. But I want to laugh. I want to have a good time. And I want to be friends with people who can laugh and let their guard down and just be themselves, because I love to laugh. I love to just lose it, on the floor rolling. And it doesn't have to be that way all the time. There are times when you want to be able to sit and talk . . .

Joanne: You draw the line at peeing in your pants because you're laughing so hard.

Robb: There are times when it's good to laugh like that and times when it's good to get at the deeper things. I wouldn't want people to look at me as being one-sided, and it can look that way because, like, "Robb is always laughing and nothing is ever wrong and that's our relationship." No, I want both sides of that. And I had it in college and I still have that now with a couple of guys individually, but we don't have that as a group and I miss that a lot. Being able to get together and hang out . . .

Joanne: And run the whole gamut of emotions. I want to laugh and then I want to cry, and then I want to laugh some more and . . .

Rebecca: And there needs to be that underlying unconditional acceptance along with that accountability, which was a huge piece of what was obviously missing with my relationships. There was not the unconditional acceptance I thought there was. Because I am so afraid to have other people judging me, I try not to judge other people so much. Like the girls in high school who told me, "I don't want to be your friend anymore." I said, "You know what, you guys? I know I didn't do anything to you and I know I'm not the weird person that you think I am. If you want to be my friend later I'll still be your friend." And that's what happened. We became friends, but those two stopped being friends with each other because that unconditional acceptance was not there between them. But it was an element that really came in handy later. And it's not like I'm great friends with them anymore, but it was really important to me that I show them what they said was not okay, but in a real friendship, here's what happens. You say what you feel like, but then you're still there.

Joanne: Because you can't have that accountability without that unconditional acceptance. There are things that Toben has said to me in the past that — without that acceptance — would have destroyed me. And I know I can tell my good friends, "You know I really hate it when you do this. I don't like you very much right now." I can do that, and I can handle having someone say that to me.

Toben: You can't have accountability without acceptance because then when someone challenges you on something, if you decide not to change or do something about it, then you really can't be friends anymore. It becomes an ultimatum.

Sarah: Here's your biggest flaw, and I can't stand you.

Joanne: It always works out better when someone can say, "I think this thing is going on with you and I have really struggled with that in the past, and here's how I dealt with it. If that sounds right to you and you want to do something about it, I'm here to work through it with you." Mostly it seems like people want you to go away and change yourself and then come back when you're all fixed up.

Robb: The motivations are totally different behind why you are saying what you're saying. If you're saying it to hurt someone, it's completely different from telling people you want to be honest with them and that you want to help them. And regardless of what happens, to let them know that you are still there for them.

Q: Time is such a big factor in all of this because it takes so much time to get to know someone well enough where you can have those kinds of conversations. How do you test those boundaries or get to the point where you can have that kind of honest interaction? It takes a long, long time before you're close enough to someone to call him a jerk . . .

Steve: For me it takes about five minutes.

Sarah: But it does, you're right. It takes a long time to get there.

Q: For me, when I think about how long it takes to develop those kinds of relationships, I think at some point it's easier to just not reach out. But it's my biggest frustration too. Why am I here all by myself?

Joanne: It goes back to that greatest desire/greatest fear thing.

Q: It feels like a vicious circle.

Michelle: It's a risk. You risk your time and your investment in a relationship for something that may or may not turn out to be something that's beneficial to you or that other person.

Joanne: A lot of times when you talk about values and opinions it helps to define some terms, because people may say the same thing and it may mean two different things, or they may make different statements and mean the same things. Like the concept of tolerance. What does that mean to you?

Toben: I think it means putting up with everybody's differences. Not that you necessarily agree with them or you like what they're doing, but you "tolerate" it.

Rebecca: I think it has to do more specifically with how you relate to people who are different from you.

Sarah: I think about it like I have a high tolerance for pain, so if I break my arm I'm not necessarily going to go into convulsions. I also think about fault tolerance. How many things can go wrong and you're still up and running?

Joanne: How does that affect your daily life?

Sarah: The worst stuff happens to me, and I just shut down. I just don't feel it. Other times, the worst crap can happen and I'll be like, "I'm fine. Everybody's fine!"

Robb: But is it really?

Sarah: That's what my therapist always asks me.

Robb: If you really think about it, tolerance means you get to a certain point – your breaking point. And if your breaking point is that – not dealing with it – it's a matter of tolerance.

Sarah: But I think my breaking point is quite a bit higher than what I've seen most other people's to be. A lot of things can go really wrong during a day and I'll be able to roll with it. It's when the really big stuff starts to happen . . . there are about two or three things that can happen that take me over the edge and I just want to crawl into the corner.

Toben: What's important to you?

Sarah: In life?

Toben: Whatever, just answer the question any way you want to.

119

Sarah: Honesty. Integrity. Having friends and having fun with my friends is very important to me. But the most important things are honesty and integrity in relationships.

Q: What keeps coming to mind is honesty.

Rebecca: That's a very broad question. I think there's a lot that's important to me and it's hard to package up all those things into words.

Toben: I want to know what the things are that matter most. Like for me, relationships are it. The relationships I have with other people help to define who I am and how I feel like I'm doing. An awful lot of things can go terribly wrong, but if everything is still okay between Joanne and me, then everything that really matters is still okay. God is important. To me, golf is important. Time and money and possessions are all important to me. But the number one thing is relationships. People are more important than things.

Michelle: I think in line with the most important things for me are to love and sacrifice for others. I think that what I have in my marriage and in my other relationships and for God are the most important things. Everything else can fall away besides that. If I keep those things in order . . .

Q: If I had to boil it down to the essentials, then my faith would be the most important thing. I know that sounds so trite.

People might think, *Here is this guy sitting around with his friends and all he can think of is "faith"?* But that's what I would defend the most. It's what I wouldn't compromise.

Steve: I would like to be able to say that, and maybe I could, but I wouldn't mean it.

Sarah: But if you can say it and mean it then . . .

Steve: . . . then that's great and maybe how it's supposed to be.

Joanne: I think it's interesting that this is kind of a hard thing to talk about. I'm wondering if it's because so often when you talk about your values and opinions, the things that are important to you, you expect people to disagree with you. Is it because values and opinions are so subjective that it's hard to give a definitive answer?

Robb: I think that's right! When we started to get into talking about these things my first thought was, "Okay, here we go." That probably stems from the fact that right now I'm in grad school with people who think very differently from the way I do. And if you voice your opinion and can't back it up, then you're blown out of the water. So when you asked me what was important to me it was family and my relationships—those were on the top. And those are things I don't really have to back up or defend to anyone. But when you first asked the question, I was totally on the defensive.

Toben: Were you worried that someone was going to ask you if you are a Democrat or a Republican?

Robb: Not so much that. I guess I'm around so many people who constantly challenge everything I say or they feel total freedom to tell me that I'm wrong, and why. And all they're really doing is voicing their opinion. It's so confrontational. If you can't defend it then obviously it isn't something that's important to you or that you've thought about very much. In this situation I can say what I think or feel, and I know I'm not going to get jumped on or have to create some elaborate defense. But I'm not used to being in a setting where that's okay.

Sarah: The word *why* is a word that seems to automatically put people on the defensive. When someone asks you why, your first tendency is to say, "Back off! That's just how I feel." That's one of the interesting things that comes from sharing with people you really want to hang out with or who you feel are safe to tell your story to. Even some of those people are going to ask the "why" question, and it's then that you have to be able to discern what they mean when they ask — either they want to judge you or they want to know you better. They want to know more about your values and opinions. There's so much to why we value the things we do, and if people ask the question and you feel like

you have to have some great defense for your answer, it's not going to happen. But if you have the desire to get to know them and share all those things that have gone into forming that value, then they would get it.

Joanne: So how do other people get to know what you value?

Robb: By watching how you live.

Toben: It's all about the choices you make. Your choices reflect what you value. Sometimes that's apparent to other people and sometimes it's not. A lot of times the things we do are done for personal or private reasons that you wouldn't want to share with anyone. People don't know what's behind what I do. But if I have a choice to go play golf or to help Steve and Michelle move, the choice that I make would reflect a value. I either value my friends over my own leisure time or I don't. If Sarah calls and I blow her off, then that communicates a value.

Rebecca: I think another way people know what you value is how you talk about other people. Not necessarily how you talk to their faces, but how you talk *about* other people. I know I've gotten myself in trouble a lot by making value judgments on other people to somebody that I'm talking with, and then that becomes a judgment rather than an effective way to express what I think. The person I'm talking to knows what I value and how that compares to someone else's values, but that's not the best way to express it.

Toben: And the other thing is that when you hear someone talk negatively about someone else behind their back, then you always wonder, "Does she talk that way about me when I'm not around?"

Q: In my case, I screw up all the time. I can articulate what I value – my faith – but it's not like it governs my life to the extent that I wish it would or even to the extent that it would be clear to those who are around me that it does matter to me so much. That doesn't mean that I don't place the highest value on it, but I also understand my own struggles and my own crap.

Toben: So how do you come to peace with the things you say you value and the way you live? When I say I value relationships, but then I don't live that out, how do you process that?

Q: It's a journey. You go in that direction. If you say you value relationships but you never develop your friendships, then that's one thing. But saying, "This is who I am every day – this is the everyday me," and saying, "This is what I value," are two different things.

Rebecca: What you say you value and what you do are two different things because what you say you value is what you intend to do. It's what we're working toward. If we determined what we value solely by what

we do, then most of us would say, "My values are selfishness and lots of money and I don't care about other people."

Sarah: Or you'd have to say that you valued work the most because it seems like that's what we do the most. We put so much time into it. Everybody would have to put work at the top of the list.

Toben: Why is it important to be able to articulate what you really do value?

Sarah: So you know where you're going. We've all talked about our futures and it just seeps out – "I want joy in my life." And I know there's a measure of joy in my life, but there would be more of it if I didn't do the job I do now. Or I would be able to live with more honesty and integrity for myself if I wasn't doing a job that I hated. So it goes back to being able to articulate your values so that you can make decisions on career path, life path, how you'll raise your kids, all that kind of stuff.

Q: I think that's why the "why" question can be so hard, because you have to explain the difference between who you are, what you value, and what you do every day. Values kind of define who we wish we were or how we wish things were.

Toben: I also think it's important to be able to articulate those values to your friends because it allows for a level of accountability. If my friends know how I desire to be and they see me doing something or living some way that isn't consistent—because I've told them what I value—they can call me on it. They can say, "Here's what you said is important to you, but here's how you're living. Explain to me how those two things go together."

Joanne: A big part of living out values and opinions is conflict. I think it would be interesting to know for myself—when I get into a situation where there's a conflict between what I value or what my opinion is and someone else's. How do I handle those things? Based on the way I think, I'm right. But the person I'm talking with may be equally convinced that they're right. Politics, homosexuality, abortion—there are all these issues that are so value-laden. And I think there is a right and a wrong for some things, but for a lot of people it comes down to opinions. So how do you handle that?

Toben: I've learned, unfortunately sometimes, that my value of relationships goes out the window when it comes to defending my opinion. I go at it to win. If I express an opinion and someone challenges it, my values and my opinions un-dock from each other at that point, and my desire is to win.

Robb: But are you winning?

Toben: No, and that's the point.

Robb: So it's a never-ending battle. You're never going to win.

Toben: It's a losing situation.

Robb: I think a lot of people go about it that way.

Toben: Sure. But as soon as I click into that mode, there's no desire to help someone think about an issue in a different way.

Joanne: Give me an example. Like I know that when you were a kid your family would have these huge discussions and everyone would be going at it to win. What was that like?

Toben: It's all motivated by selfishness, by wanting to appear intelligent, and by wanting to get your way. When it comes to a lot of things, like Christianity for example, when you express your opinion, people act like, "How can you be so uneducated as to think that?" So that's the way it's always been in my family. When I was young, I wanted some cap guns, and my parents didn't want to buy me guns because they were morally opposed to them. So I built this huge case about how guns were important to my development as a child. And they ended up going for it. And that was the first time I ever argued my way into something that I wanted. That started a pattern of behavior that's still with me today. I'm trying to get better about it, but I guess it comes down to realizing that no one is going to change the mind of another person, who holds to an opposite opinion, just through words. I don't think it happens.

Joanne: If you're in a relationship with someone and you trust them, then maybe what they say does make a difference or could help you change your mind about something.

Toben: Sure, because I could see that person live out what they were talking about.

Sarah: Yeah, someone saying, "This made a real difference for me, blah, blah, blah," could influence me to try something different or look somewhere for help.

Joanne: Our opinions can change. But do our values change? And if not, what's the difference between values and opinions?

Rebecca: I think values definitely change. I mean, look how different you are now than when you were in adolescence. Your values are totally different now than they were then. Partially they're from your parents and partially they're your own, but they change drastically by the time you become an adult.

Sarah: And it's shaped by your experiences growing up. Once you get to be an adult there's not a lot of stuff that happens to you that will change your values because your values are set in place. Then your values inform your opinions.

Rebecca: Especially because everything you do is centered around what those values are.

Q: When you become an adult, that's when all your values are challenged. Not so much as a kid, because they're not really your values—they're your family's. It's how you grew up, and you understand it but you don't necessarily own them. But as you become an adult, all of those things are challenged and you sift through what you really believe—what is going to stay and what is going to go—and you turn out to be a different person.

Toben: I think that's the time when your values are most radically changed. Probably more than at any other time in your life is when the rubber meets the road and somebody asks you "Why?" for the first time. I mean you can go the whole way through high school and even into college—or depending on what kind of college, all the way through college—without ever being challenged, because you're with other people who are like you. In your hometown, at your college, because you've made the choice to be there with people who have made a similar choice to be there or whatever. I think when you finally get out to a place where somebody asks you the why, that's when those values start having implications.

Sarah: Voting. I remember when I was able to vote, I really had to question how my values informed my opinions as I asked myself, "How am I going to vote in this election?" I'm not going to go in there and check off boxes. Career choice is another one.

Toben: It's complicated.

Robb: Yeah, one of my thoughts in talking about values and opinions and things is that if you're talking to someone, thinking you're going to change his or her mind, it forms a whole new way of looking at things. But if you go to the table knowing that you're not here to change the person's mind, you're here just to talk about different values, opinions, and things. But more often than not, people are trying to change everyone else, and as a result, people don't listen to each other. And when people don't listen to each other, that's when they get pissed off. And when I'm supposed to be listening to you, I'm thinking of rebuttals and what I can stack up in my defense. And that's not a normal conversation. A normal conversation is listening and learning and trying to understand why the person thinks that. "So this happened to you. I can understand why you think that. That's never happened to me. This is why I believe what I believe." I think too often—even in politics and everything—people go to the table with background information, lawyers go to the table getting things handed to them with reasons why, and no one's listening to each other. And I think if you come to the table with that type of thought, you're not going to get very far and you're going to be pretty close-minded.

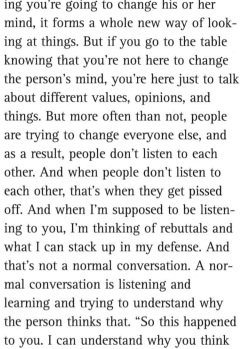

Sarah: And I think that's what we end up being. We end up saying, "Here's my list of values and opinions. Tick off the ones you agree with, and if you agree with enough boxes I'll be your friend." Instead of saying, "Let's sit down and talk about what we value and why. Here's my opinion on certain subjects; what do you think?" I totally appreciate that.

I had a friend in college and we sat down one time and made a list of all the things we believed the total opposite on. It ran the gamut—all the way from abortion to politics. At the end we laughed about it, and we kept that list to remind us that even though we had all these totally different opinions, we could still be friends and listen to each other and talk about those things. That was not going to be the defining moment of our friendship—whether or not we agreed on certain things.

Robb: How else are we supposed to learn? We stop learning when we stop listening.

Sarah: Right.

Robb: That seems horrible to me. To take where I am right now and completely stop the learning process would be awful. But to think, gosh, look at all the things I continue to learn that I may not agree with—even walking away—but at least I have a clearer picture of what people are going through and what's out there.

Q: If I've got an opinion or a value based on a life experience I faced as an adult, it was a challenge for me, and now it's a value that I hold dear; and then if someone else has a different opinion on that same thing, I think it's very difficult for me to let those things be challenged. Because it's devaluing my own experience. I mean, the reason I hold this dear is because of some experience that I've had. And now you're saying that I'm totally wrong in my conclusion based on my own experience. And I think that goes both ways. As we're talking to others, we have to realize their values may be based on their own experience.

Toben: Because you only see the face of it, you don't see its formation. We do that all the time when people express their opinions. We attack the opinion or the value without taking the time to find out why it is they hold that value or opinion. And I think if we did take the time, it would totally transform the way we interact with them. If you understood this is their opinion because they were abused as a child, or this is something they value because they grew up so poor, or whatever, then we wouldn't attack their value, because we would understand where it came from. And that doesn't mean that we wouldn't want to work with them or engage with them, but at least it wouldn't be this attacking.

Robb: It brings a personal side to it which, when you're arguing, you don't want. You don't want the personal side because that will make you stop and think. But we need that.

Toben: Plus, it helps you understand why somebody can't just change his mind. You can't just argue and somehow the words you say are going to override twenty years . . .

Robb: Or take that experience away.

Toben: "Oh, I'm sorry your dad did that to you, but here's two or three things that should just spin you right around on that." That just doesn't happen.

Q: Or, "How could you believe that way?"

Joanne: When I think about my values and opinions, I think they're most obviously challenged or disagreed with in general ways. Like in the media I see things that go against what I value, things I disagree with that aren't my opinion. I don't know that my opinions or my values on big things get challenged often in a more personal way. I'm wondering if that's your experience too? I listen to you, Sarah, talk about your friend in college and how you disagreed about so many things. I think I need more friends like that!

"Doing a 180"

Think back to a time when you've changed your mind about a particular value or changed your mind on an issue. What caused the change? Was it reading something, talking with someone, or an experience you had? What does your experience teach you about how values and opinions get changed?

"Agreeing to Disagree"

Are there people in your life that you disagree with about major issues—
things like politics, abortion, or euthanasia? How has that affected your relationship?
Your own values and opinions?

"Why?"

"Why?" can be a threatening question—especially in a heated discussion.
When you're asked why you think the way you do, do you tend to respond with a
"just because" or do you tell the story that shaped your opinion? When you ask others
why, do you stop to listen to the story behind their opinions? How can you listen to
others more carefully in the future?

PART FIVE:
WHAT I BELIEVE
STORIES ABOUT FAITH

faith \fāth\ *n* **1**: belief

and trust in and loyalty

to God **2**: firm belief in

something for which

there is no proof

"Now faith is being sure of what we hope for, and certain of what we do not see," wrote the writer of Hebrews in the Bible. We all have faith in something. Gravity. Love. Wind. Power. God.

I (Joanne) think that faith is one of the most central things about who we are as people. More than anything, it defines us. What we have faith in might be found in the answer to this question: "If you don't believe in anything strongly enough to die for it, do you really have anything worth living for?"

Faith may not always dictate how we live. After all, we are human. But faith, beliefs, ideals are something we strive for. What we believe directs our paths—even if we stray from them.

For me, faith is intensely personal. It's about my relationship with God—something that lives deep inside of me in a place I can't define with words or prove with my senses.

Sometimes I have a hard time talking with my friends about what I believe. I want to tell them what it is that I'd die for, what makes my life worth living, but I'm not sure where to start. I'm not sure what words to use—if there are words that would adequately express my meaning. At the heart of it, I'm afraid of how my friends would react. I don't want them to think I'm close-minded, part of the ultra-conservative religious right, or any number of other descriptions floating around in the culture.

The more I think about it, the more I think I have to tell others about my faith with stories. Why God is sometimes the only thing that holds my marriage together. Why prayer doesn't feel like a hollow exercise to me. Why I believe what I do. Why I know in my heart it's true—even though there's no proof.

We live out our faith in the stories of our lives. Those beliefs motivate our actions. While we were students at Whitworth college, two guys started a student organization called En Cristo out of their belief that we should care for the homeless. They began visiting the homeless once a week, just to spend time with them and be their friends. More people started going with them. Then they began taking food along. Soon, other students spent an afternoon each week packing sack lunches. More students showed up to help deliver them. Within a few months, En Cristo was the biggest club on campus as more and more students shared the belief that they could make a difference in the lives of the homeless in our city.

What do you believe in? What are things you know without proof? Sharing your beliefs with others can be the scariest thing of all.

God
Jesus
People
Rituals
Heaven
The sacred
Church
Religion
Angels
Goodness
Obedience
Prayer
Ceremony
Faith
Spirituality
Hope
Love
Holiness
Mercy
Forgiveness
Character
The Bible

The world in my eyes...

Just as rose-colored glasses turn the world pink, faith colors how we see the world. Ask ten people what heaven is like, and you'll most likely get ten very different answers. So what do you think of when you hear the words from the following list?

God	Angels	Love
Jesus	Goodness	Holiness
People	Obedience	Mercy
Rituals	Prayer	Forgiveness
Heaven	Ceremony	Character
The sacred	Faith	The Bible
Church	Spirituality	
Religion	Hope	

"RULING THINGS OUT"

by Jim Hancock

I

I've spent most of my life ruling things out. It's slow, painstaking work, weeding out things that look promising but don't produce. Some things—especially spiritual things—have deep roots and come out hard. But it has to be done. Weeds grow up ugly.

I'm not alone in this. I have a friend who grew up without religion. Having no reason to value one kind of spirituality over another, she tried the salad-bar approach, sampling this and that, looking for something nourishing. The menu was pretty thin by the time she got to the Self-Realization Fellowship. And it wasn't long before she said, "Well, that wasn't it either," and moved down the line to a church that identified itself as "Christian." She wasn't even sure what a Christian was, but that's where she found the meal she was hungry for.

Another friend landed among Christians when she could no longer justify her career as a self-help seminar leader. The money was still there but she felt like a whore—selling slogans that held no meaning for her own life. Should an emotional/relational/spiritual failure take money for telling other people how to live? Not an unreasonable question. She gave up the money and found some followers of Christ with more hard questions than easy answers. And she seems to have found her soul.

I know another guy who woke up one day to realize he spent his days not doing drugs and his nights wondering if it was worth it. He was sober but far from satisfied. He's a Twelve-Stepper, this friend, so he did what those guys do when they feel stuck: He went back to the beginning. *Step Three: We decide to turn our will and our life over to God as we understand him.* This launched my friend on a quest to find the name of his higher power.

The name, it turned out, was familiar, but he hardly recognized the face. The Jesus he came to believe in as an adult bore little resemblance to the Jesus of his childhood.

Me too. On the surface, my life is not much like these friends. I've never had much of an appetite for controlled substances—though I've used food like a drug. I guess I must've been looking the other way when the self-help thing blew through town. And boy, did I grow up with religion.

Still, underneath I don't think I'm very different.

Maybe it's enough to say I'm the son of a Southern Baptist preacher. Perhaps not.

The vocabulary of my early years was the language of the churches my father served: Sunday school, Training Union, Royal Ambassadors, study courses, Watch Night Service, prayer meeting, and, every so often, revivals. These terms have unmistakable meaning to me, though they may be gibberish to you, and with them comes a dictionary of jargon: saved, converted, washed in the blood, baptized, filled with the Spirit, sanctified, declared righteous, made holy.

My understanding of holiness was shaped by revivals—those week-long attempts to spark a fire in the lives of people who, as far as I could see, were already pretty holy. (Is that right? Can I modify the word *holy?* Is pretty holy like fairly unique?)

Revivals worked like this: An out-of-town preacher performed the functions my father filled every week as pastor. Each evening, this hired gun delivered a sermon designed to get people out of their seats, to come forward, to receive Jesus as Savior and Lord, to surrender their lives to Christ. These were moments of high emotion. Church members brought "unsaved" friends and neighbors. All through the week, the preacher and the pastor dropped by to visit people—mostly stay-at-home moms and the unemployed, I suppose. I recall tagging along on some of those awkward visits.

Each night of the revival, the visiting preacher delivered one of his seven best sermons. I believe this is true because, when he did revival preaching, my dad took only the notes from his surefire winners. I suppose that's no different from a lecturer on the university circuit, but I remember thinking it seemed a little like cheating.

The point was to get people to come forward and, by golly, people did. They came a few at a time early in the week, but the number grew as the days passed. They responded to the call for commitment to Christ, or rededication of their lives to Christ, or to move their Letter (code for jumping from one church to another). All this with tears or tight-jawed determination. "This time I mean it."

I never was aware they didn't mean it. They seemed pretty holy to me already.

As much as revivals shaped my understanding of holiness, prayer meeting shaped my understanding of the daily grind. Each Wednesday night (unless there was a revival) there was prayer meeting. The prayer meeting crowd was never as large as Sunday night church, which was never as large as Sunday morning worship.

Did I mention Sunday night church? The Sunday night lineup was: five o'clock choir practice, a light supper at six, Baptist Training Union from six-thirty to seven-fifteen, Sunday night church (where the youth choir sang) from seven-thirty to eight-thirty. Then, if there was anybody to run it, youth fellow-ship from eight-thirty to nine-thirty or thereabouts. A full day on top of Sunday school and church.

One result of all this churchgoing is that I was exposed to a serious amount of the Bible. Another byproduct—a nonexperience actually—is that I didn't see *The Wizard of Oz* until I was in my thirties. I was keenly aware of missing that remarkable film because CBS showed *Oz* in prime time every spring of my childhood. They ran it early so families could watch it together and still get the little ones to bed at a decent hour. But they always played it on Sunday night so I saw the first twenty minutes of *The Wizard of Oz* over and over—right up to the moment when the house lands on the Witch, and Dorothy knows before she says it that she's not in Kansas anymore. Then we left for church. And that was that. Once or twice I considered claiming I was sick, but I didn't think I could stand the guilt.

But it was Wednesday when I interrupted myself and I was on my way to prayer meeting. Prayer meeting was the elite. And the bored. The elite came to church on Wednesday night because that's what a good Christian would do. The bored came for obvious reasons.

After singing a few prayer meeting favorites like "In the Garden" and "Sweet Hour of Prayer" the pastor, Dad, led a brief devotional, then invited prayer requests. The nature of those requests strikes me even now. Alcoholism and other family craziness. Husbands and sons out of work. Sick fathers and mothers. The building program. The coming revival. Traveling mercies. Grief. Concerns for the lukewarm and indifferent—two classes of people, I think, but pronounced as one word.

When it appeared the well was dry, a long pause. Then—most curious now that I think about it—my father asked for unspoken requests. Several people would raise a hand shoulder high. He always nodded as if he knew why these requests must remain unspoken. And maybe he did. God knows he had unspoken needs of his own.

What were these unspoken requests? What behavior was so bad it couldn't be mentioned at church? What shame was too deep for words? What hurt so awfully that saying it out loud was to risk hemorrhaging?

To this day it is unspoken requests that capture my imagination. I ruled out Sunday night church as my friend ruled out the Self-Realization Fellowship, because that wasn't it. I gave up BTU and choir as my friend gave up her motivational seminar tour, not because these are bad but because they failed to make me good.

What I can't seem to rule out is the God of unspoken requests. I believe that's where the real stuff always was, and is. Real need, real brokenness, real hunger. Then and now, theirs and mine.

I've generated more than a few unspoken requests myself. Dare I cling to wild, irrational hope that God knows those things and might actually do something about them? God, how I want to open my mouth and say my unspoken requests out loud, to speak the unspeakable because that's where God is real if God is real anywhere at all.

II

Before Calland Dalrymple, there was football.

These days I'm likely to work or read a book during the Super Bowl, pausing to watch the commercials. But when I was a kid, football was my god.

Given the choice between public school and a cutting-edge private school at Florida State University, my only question had to do with the quality of their football programs. Don't ever say I wasn't devoted to The Game.

Still, in tenth grade Calland Dalrymple challenged my religion. Calland was going out with Thorne Caldwell, but I couldn't imagine it would last. I waited, memorizing her face across the lunch room.

When she gave Caldwell the boot, I had little choice but to worship her. I think I'd heard that no one can serve two masters, but for several months between the end of my sophomore football season and the beginning of my junior year, I tried. Spring training was a challenge, but I made it without estranging Calland or football. Then it was summer and I was free.

Age was a complicating factor. I was not yet sixteen so there was plenty of telephone work early on. I turned sixteen on July 7 and rushed to the Department of Motor Vehicles for the test that would gain me the license to date Calland Dalrymple at will.

Well, not quite at will. Calland's parents were uncomfortable with the intensity of my devotion. I was with her every day, several times a day—all day if I could arrange it. Mr. and Mrs. Dalrymple thought it was too much. What can I say?

On August 10, things changed. Finishing the most successful year of my life, I felt like a failure. I didn't know why. Everything from football to Calland Dalrymple was as good as I could imagine, and still I felt unsatisfied, inept, empty.

I was at summer camp when the lights came on and I saw Jesus as if for the first time. This was no revival. It wasn't Sunday school or prayer meeting. It was a new hope that Jesus could make me stop feeling empty.

My prayer was inelegant. Informed by the failure of my success, I said, "I feel like I've messed up everything I've ever done. I don't know if you can do anything with me, but you're welcome to try." Not much there.

It must have been enough. Abruptly, I awoke to things I knew about but never experienced.

I talked to God exuberantly, desperately, continuously about anything and everything. I learned to drive and pray at the same time, with my eyes open—a character flaw that persists to the present. I kept at it because, unlikely as it seemed, for the first time in my life I thought God was listening.

I couldn't get enough of the Bible. It started making sense, not because I understood everything but because I understood *anything*.

Something emerged like a conscience but without the nagging. I had a growing sense about right and wrong. A month into my junior year I took Patty Hicks to a dance. When the music slowed, without thinking, I embraced her and slid my hands down onto her bottom—an old dancing habit. Patty removed her hands from my shoulders and removed my hands from her behind. I laughed to myself in the dark. *She's not a Christian,* I thought, *and she's correcting my behavior. This is really cool!*

But that was months later, after I did a good thing and a bad thing. Both were difficult.

I could tell this new thing with Jesus would not be denied. Experience told me football was a jealous god. I wasn't sure I could play football without worshiping it. Well then, I would just have to quit. Heresy! But I meant it. I gave it two weeks.

Two weeks turned into two years; it turned out I was a better ball player when football was a game and not a religion. I don't know why I was surprised.

My changing attitude dismayed the coaches at first: "You're complacent, Hancock!" But they couldn't argue with results. I displaced a senior in the starting lineup, and the rest of my football career was about as good as it could have been.

I wish I could say that about the rest of my relationship with Calland Dalrymple. I knew things were different, but I couldn't get the same perspective with Calland that I got with football. The truth is I wimped out. I'm humiliated to say it; I regret it and I wish I could take it back. I just stopped calling. I'm sorry.

I saw Calland after college in what looked like a wonderful relationship with Lee Meadows. I felt awkward, wanted to apologize. I kept silent because of the others in the room.

What would I have said? Not enough probably. She didn't ask to be my god. She was never meant to be worshiped. Maybe I didn't know that then. Probably I did.

III

When I finally broke the silence, I thought I might lose my job. But I couldn't keep quiet any longer.

I suppose the story begins in high school, about a year after the lights came on. I was mowing the lawn one afternoon when it occurred to me that my sexual behavior was out of line. It wasn't illegal but it was lust-driven. I hadn't thought much about it, but when it came to mind that day, I saw it for what it was and I wanted no part of it. "I don't ever wanna do that again," I said and really meant it.

And God responded by wiping that slate clean. I didn't struggle, I didn't even think about it. It was gone. A miracle if you ask me.

About ten years later I realized, like it or not, that sexual compulsion was back and badder than ever. I was angry. God offered such immediate relief when I was seventeen and a new believer. Why would God give it back now? I set my jaw and determined I would muscle my way through this. If God wasn't going to deal with it, I would have to, out of love and obedience and self-discipline.

I failed.

God, I failed over and over. Sometimes I equivocated, sometimes I was caught by surprise, sometimes I was seduced by desire, sometimes I was just worn down. But always, sooner than later, I failed. And with every failure I felt more isolated, less real.

That wasn't all. I used food as a drug. I ate when I felt sad or angry or tired or elated. It wasn't about hunger; I ate for any reason or no reason at all. Of course, the more I ate the fatter I got and the more isolated I felt.

That wasn't all. I worked ridiculous hours attempting to make people love me. I was an approval junkie, making promises I couldn't keep without sacrificing my personal life—which was okay by me.

I felt tense at home. I felt ashamed for the way I treated my wife and daughter. I wasn't making progress against my sexual compulsion, and I was gaining weight. I was angry and sarcastic. I felt powerless and afraid to change. And more isolated.

That wasn't all. I was in debt. I spent money like I ate—comfort in my lows and elevation for my highs. Only it wasn't money, it was credit. I came up with a thousand reasons for spending more than I earned. The bottom line was more debt.

That wasn't all. I turned into a liar. Approval junkies are liars by nature, I think. It is, as my friend Toben says, "the truth, plus or minus 10 percent." Whatever it takes to spin the transaction in my favor.

One afternoon, a friend confided his struggle with a sexual compulsion that had him feeling guilty and isolated. You can't imagine how sympathetic I was with my head-nodding and gentle murmurs of understanding.

It was a lie. His compulsion was the same as mine. I wasn't feeling sympathy, I was feeling empathy. We shared a weakness. I knew so much about his struggle because it was so much like mine. I could have comforted him, he could have comforted me. It didn't happen because I wimped out—again. I remained silent and we both left alone.

Sex, food, approval, anger, sarcasm, spending, lying. These are on the list of things I had to come clean about or die. I was working with adolescents and their families in a church. I thought honesty about these things might put a stop to that employment, but I couldn't keep quiet another day.

So I began telling the truth. I didn't just blurt it all out one day. I made the truth part of each day. I stopped pretending. I started answering honestly, even when the truth terrified me. In a word play on John 8:32, Carlisle Barney said: "You will know the truth and the truth will make you flinch before it sets you free." Yep, that's it exactly.

I'm not saying I'm worse than the next guy, I'm saying I'm not what I appear to be. I'm saying if I were going to get better I would have by now.

I'm not going to get better. If Jesus doesn't show up to energize me today, I'll fail any one of a dozen ways. It's inevitable. I need the presence of Jesus like I need air. Without him I think I'd suffocate. I know I'd fail.

The happy byproduct of all this is that, apart from my own goodness I assure you, I'm not locked in sexual compulsion today. I lost fifty pounds. I'm getting out of debt because I'm not spending to ease my pain. I'm learning to express anger more appropriately, and I'm far less likely to lie (though I'm tempted to do it every day). What I couldn't—and probably wouldn't—do for myself, Jesus is doing for me and through me.

I didn't lose my job. In fact, I got better at my job, just as I was a better athlete when I learned to play football instead of worshiping the game.

What I'm ruling out these days, finally, is me. Not me as a person but me as a god.

I've never really been mad at God; God just has the job I want.

Actually that's only partly true. I've been deeply angry with God because God has the job I want. And because I feel so unhappy that I'm so underqualified for the job if I could get it. I long to be in control of something. I want to bring something to the party, to be a player. Ultimately, I guess I want God to be obligated to me.

That's not how it works. The river runs to the sea, not to feed the sea, but because that's where the river comes from. Bit by bit, I'm starting to not be so mad about that. There's an hour now and again when I even enjoy it.

So the second miracle is greater than the first. What I wanted was freedom from weakness and, honestly, independence from Jesus. What I got is greater dependence on Jesus than I ever wanted. And with the dependence, growing intimacy. That's what I would really have wanted if I'd only known. .

Jim says he's spent most of his life "ruling things out." Have you ever felt like that? What are some of the things you've ruled out as you've grown older?

What was your experience of religion when you were growing up? How did it affect you?

Have you ever been really mad at God? Why? What did you do about it?

"I began telling the truth." Can you think of a time when you determined to tell the truth like Jim did?

Jim says without Jesus he'd suffocate and fail. What do you think of his statement?

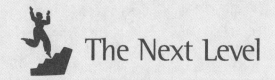# The Next Level

Do you think this statement by P. J. Bailey is accurate: "Faith is a higher faculty than reason"?

Douglas Coupland has said that Generation X is the first generation "raised without religion." Do you think he's right or wrong about that? Explain.

In *My Confession,* Leo Tolstoy wrote, "Faith is the force of life." Do you agree or disagree?

In national surveys, an overwhelming majority of people say they believe in God. Why do you think that is?

Do the people you know who profess a particular faith make it seem attractive or unattractive? Why?

Agree or disagree: "So long as man remains free he strives for nothing so incessantly and so painfully as to find someone to worship" (Fyodor Dostoyevski, *The Brothers Karamazov*).

Do you ever go to church? Why or why not?

Benjamin Franklin said, "The way to see by Faith is to shut the Eye of Reason." Is that good advice or not? Why?

If you could ask God anything, what would you ask him?

Do you think God hears people when they pray? Why, or why not?

Albert Camus in *The Fall* wrote, "Can one be a saint if God does not exist? That is the only concrete problem I know of today." What do you think about that?

Does God exist? How do you know?

Do you pray? Why?

"To believe in God is to yearn for His existence and, furthermore, it is to act as if He did exist" (Miguel de Unamuno). Do you think he's right? Why, or why not? Does belief in God mean acting like he exists?

What do you think God looks like?

George MacDonald wrote, "The principal part of faith is patience." What does patience have to do with faith?

What are some of the things you know without a doubt? How do you know them?

How would you respond to the following statement? "He that has lost faith, what has he left to live on?" (Publilius Syrus).

What is something that you pray for often? Why?

Emerson wrote, "We are born believing. A man bears beliefs, as a tree bears apples." Do you think he is right or wrong about that?

How would you describe prayer to someone who'd never tried it?

In her poem "Faith," Elizabeth Oakes Smith writes: "Faith is the subtle chain which binds us to the infinite; the voice of a deep life within, that will remain until we crowd it thence." What is that "infinite" thing that faith binds us to?

There's a bumper sticker that says, "Jesus, save me from your followers." Why do you think someone would express that sentiment?

What is the relationship between faith and religion?

Dr. Robert Anthony said, "If you don't change your beliefs, your life will be like this forever. Is that good news?" To what extent do you think your beliefs determine what your life is like? Why?

Shirley Temple Black said, "I stopped believing in Santa Claus when I was six. Mother took me to see him in a department store and he asked for my autograph." Have you ever lost one of your beliefs? How did it happen? How did you feel?

"No iron chain, or outward force of any kind, can ever compel the soul of a person to believe or to disbelieve" (Thomas Carlyle). If this is true, how do we influence or change others' beliefs? Is it impossible? What, then, forms our beliefs? How do you know?

In her song, "One of Us" Joan Osborn asks, if you'd want to see God if it meant you'd have to believe in him. How would you answer her?

Thomas Fuller said, "He does not believe that does not live according to his belief." Do you live according to your beliefs? How? If not, how can you bring your behavior in line with your beliefs?

"It's an indulgence to sit in a room and discuss your beliefs as if they were a juicy piece of gossip" (Lillian Hellman). Are your beliefs something you discuss often with other people? Why, or why not? Is it something you're comfortable doing, or is it difficult for you to share your beliefs?

David Jenkins said, "As I get older I seem to believe less and less and yet to believe what I do believe more and more." Which of your beliefs do you hold more tightly to as you grow older? Which ones have you let go? What's the difference between those beliefs?

"It is easier to believe than to doubt" (Everett D. Martin). Do you agree with this statement? Why, or why not? Can you share an example from your own life?

John Stuart Mill said, "One person with a belief is equal to a force of ninety-nine who have only interests." Have you ever seen this proved true? When? How would you define the difference between a belief and an interest?

"What distinguishes the majority of men from the few is their inability to act according to their beliefs" (Henry Miller). Why do you think people have a hard time acting according to their beliefs? What makes the difference for the few? Are you part of the majority or part of the few?

Olin Miller said, "To be absolutely certain about something, one must know everything or nothing about it." Do you agree with his statement? Are you certain of things that you know either nothing or everything about? Like what?

It's been said that for those who believe, no proof is necessary. But for those who don't believe, no proof is possible. Are there things you believe without proof? Things you don't believe that no evidence would convince you otherwise?

Luis Bunuel said, "If someone were to prove to me—right this minute—that God, in all his luminousness, exists, it wouldn't change a single aspect of my behavior." If someone proved the same to you, would your behavior change? How? Why?

Voltaire said that if God did not exist, it would be necessary to invent him. Do you agree with him? Why? Do you think God exists, or is he a mere invention of humankind? Why?

Martin Luther King, Jr., said, "Take the first step in faith. You don't have to see the whole staircase, just take the first step." Have you ever taken a step of faith like this? When? What was it like?

Toben: So, here's the big question. What do you believe?

Sarah: I grew up in the church and I didn't know what I believed in. And I didn't ever really get the understanding that Jesus really loved me for who I was. And that was because of double meanings that I got. If you say God really loves you for who you are, then why are you putting on fancy clothing to go to church on Sunday mornings? And I really rebelled against that and had a big, whopping fight with God from the time I was fifteen until I was probably twenty-one . . . twenty-three . . . twenty-four. I just had this big, fat battle with God over why it was that everybody would say one thing and mean something totally different. It took a long time for me to get around the fact that Christianity is not about people, and it really isn't.

I go to a church, and it's plenty screwed up, just like every other church I've ever been to. I wouldn't go away from it for all the money in the world because I think the most important thing I believe is that God loves me, that he sent Jesus, that Jesus died for me and loved me that much – unconditionally. And that no matter what I do tomorrow or the next day, I'm not going to be outside that love. Now that doesn't give me license to go run around and do a bunch of stuff. I don't think God says, "Now please go out and make it worth my while that I had Jesus come down – go out and sin a lot." But I feel like I'm more and more able to say this is who I am, unapologetically, instead of being so ashamed. I think that was the undercurrent that everything I believe came from – the fact that for such a long time I was so ashamed because everything I did, I felt, was taking me further and further away from the love of God. But now I feel like regardless of what I do, his love is not going away. It's a nice thing to have there and it's a beautiful way to live. That's where the joy comes from. I could screw up a whole bunch of times today, and I will! And I'm going to screw up a bunch of times tomorrow. And there's no reason for me to get judgmental on other people about how they're going to screw up, because I'm going to screw up too.

Michelle: I believe the most important thing for me to do is to develop my own personal, intimate relationship with God. And that above all else he wants to have that relationship with me. And if I focus on that and strive to build that relationship I will be able to communicate and reach people where they're at. And a lot of times I don't even realize that I'm doing that if my eyes are truly focused on God. And for me personally, that's what I'm going to strive to do and hope and trust that God will take care of the rest and that all my screw-ups along the way are covered by his grace.

Rebecca: I've learned, and believe, that what most people strive for is consistency and predictability, and that in doing so they put their faith in a lot of things that are extremely tenuous at times. That includes putting their faith in other people. And everything we have in this world is fallible. I mean, things we believed to be true about science and nature forty years ago, we've found out aren't true. And people put faith in those things. And so I've learned that Jesus is the only thing I can put my faith in that is completely predictable—everything he's told us has been proved true and for our own good, and it's a comforting feeling to know there's this built-in best friend who's always going to be there for you. You can test him as much as you want to and he's not going to change. It's very easy to put your faith in things here, and especially in people, and we're setting ourselves up for disappointment and failure every time. We end up disappointed and in a deep hole of despair because of it. It took my own personal experience to learn that at one point I had put my entire faith into these friends I had and this relationship I had with Robb, and all of those things came crashing down at the same time. The lesson I learned from that was the worst thing that ever happened to me, but at the same time I learned this is really stupid and I don't want to live my life feeling like everything has been so disappointing. And Jesus has shown that if you put your faith in these things, you'll be disappointed. But he's consistent. He came and died for us, and none of us could ever say we would do that. And if I have this friend in Jesus—and I wouldn't ever want to do anything to hurt him—then that's how I would try to live my life.

Q: I grew up in a church that taught it was your responsibility to hold your own in the Christian faith and that Jesus died for you because you had value and that he thought you were so good. And I always took that to believe there's so much crap in my life because I don't see the value in my life. What I've come to realize is that it's all because God loved us and we *didn't* deserve it. There's nothing about us that gives God a reason to love us or to die for us. He did it because he wanted to and because he is glorifying himself. Somehow, even in this crappy life of mine, he's getting glory, because every day I'm changing a little bit. I'm not exactly like I was the day before. Ten years from now, I'll be different from how I am now, just like ten years ago I was very different from how I am now. That's just the thing I have come to really appreciate about God and his work in my life: He's the one doing all the work, and I'm the one reaping all the benefits—even though I don't deserve it.

Robb: I grew up not really understanding what it meant that Jesus died for me, for us, for everyone—even the people I don't like being around. I remember in high school and college really trying to fathom what that meant, and trying to put it into terms of what I was going through then—like being out with a friend and if that friend pushed me out of the way and was hit by a car and killed. And how I would feel about that, and the survivor's guilt I would have. "Why me?" I'd rather die than have a friend die. What am I worth, to be living right now? I really struggled with that a lot, because I couldn't understand how anyone around me would do that for me—let alone someone who, at

the time, I didn't think really even knew me. And it's been the past year or year and a half that it's finally come to make more sense. And the power that's come to overwhelm me at times—of someone who died for me, knowing every single part of me—all the horrible things I think and do and the things I do to others. That's what keeps me going. I think of it that way, saying God chose to keep me alive this long and I need to be living my life to the fullest every day and reaching out to others and using my gifts. If I'm not doing that, if I'm looking the other way, then I'm not doing what God asked me to do. I almost look at it like having a second chance. It's like having a brush with death and saying, "Okay, now that I know I could have died, what am I going to do? How am I going to live my life to the fullest so that I can look back when I'm dying and say I know I did the best I could?" Just having that perspective makes me feel alive—that I have a second chance and no one can take that away from me. I think that is at the root of why I do what I do, and why I think the way I think.

Steve: I would agree with what Sarah said as far as screwing up a lot. I mean I screw up a lot and do a lot of things wrong. My belief system is fairly short, based on God's unconditional love and grace and forgiveness.

Joanne: When I think in terms of what I believe, I think about faith a lot. And the Bible describes faith as believing in something I can't see. And a lot of times I think that if I can't really see God, how can I keep believing? God loves us so much and asks us to have faith in him—but he *does* give us evidence. There are situations where it may look like there's no way for anything to work out and bring good to anyone, but there is evidence of things in the past. When I feel like my life is out of control and I can't handle things, when I cry out, "Where are you God? Why aren't you answering me? Why can't I feel you?" I think back to the times when I've been certain that God does care about us and he can take impossible things and work them out for good. I really believe that God loves me. Like he says, whatever goes on in my life, he knows, and as difficult as it may be, he cares about it, and in the end it's going to work out for his and my benefit. It may seem completely impossible for that to be true, but it is. That's something to hang on to when things get weird.

Toben: I've been a Christian all my life and was raised in a Christian home, and occasionally I've gotten glimpses of how I'd be without God. I've done things and seen that if it weren't for him, I'd be that way all the time. And I would do worse. I'm very convinced that if it weren't for God in my life, I'd be a miserable, selfish, abusive wounder of other people. And I'm glad that I'm not that way and that in those times when I do those things or act out those behaviors that I'm forgiven. That sums it up for me.

"Faith and Actions"

How does what you believe influence your actions?
Are there things you do just because you believe they're the right thing to do?

"I Believe . . ."

How would you sum up what you believe?
How does that affect your everyday life?

"God"

Do you believe in God? Why, or why not? What do you think he's like?
What has influenced your opinions of God?
How does believing (or not believing) in God affect your life?

ABOUT THE AUTHORS

TOBEN and JOANNE HEIM met in high school and were engaged to be married the night before Joanne graduated. They went to Whitworth College in Spokane, Washington, got married halfway through school, and moved to France after graduation. In Paris, Joanne worked for a French software company and Toben learned to be alone and like it.

They moved to Colorado Springs and both started working at NavPress Publishing Group, where Toben is the trade sales manager and Joanne was an editor. She now is a full-time mom for their daughter, Audrey, and two miniature beagles, Daisy and Abigail. This is their first book.

Improve your relationships.

You know exactly what you want in a relationship. So why do you always end up with someone completely wrong for you? *Victim of Love?* examines unhealthy relationships and shows how to break bad cycles.
Victim of Love (Tom Whiteman & Randy Peterson) $13

Looking for creative ways to romance your spouse? Discover these fun, unique ideas to show your husband how much you love and appreciate him each day of the year.
How to Be Your Husband's Best Friend (Dan Bolin & John Trent) $6

In need of new ideas to tell your wife you love her? Use these 365 fun and creative ways to show your wife how you feel about her.
How to Be Your Wife's Best Friend (Cay Bolin & Cindy Trent) $6

Become a friend—someone your son loves spending time with. Use these 365 ways to connect with your son.
How to Be Your Little Man's Dad (Dan Bolin & Ken Sutterfield) $6

Become that special someone in your daughter's life. Use these fun and creative ways to show her you care and deepen your relationship.
How to Be Your Daughter's Daddy (Dan Bolin) $6

Get your copies today at your local bookstore or call (800) 366-7788 and ask for offer **#2297**.

PIÑON PRESS